THE   BOOK   OF

Cake
Decorating

THE   BOOK   OF

Cake
Decorating

WENDY DUFALL

Photography by
PHILIP WALKER

TED SMART

Specially produced for Ted Smart,
Guardian House, Borough Road, Godalming, Surrey GU7 2AE.

ISBN 1 85613 109 2

This book was created by Pegasus Editions Limited,
Premier House, Hinton Road, Bournemouth, Dorset BH1 2EF

Editor: Hilary Walden
Designer: Paul Baker
Home Economists: Carla Seymour, Louise Holloway, Karen Pearman
Photographer: Philip Walker
Typeset by: Shirley Westerhoff
Colour separations by: Aero Offset (Bournemouth) Limited
Printed in Belgium by: Proost International Book Production,
Turnhout, Belgium

Notes:
All spoon measurements are equal.
1 teaspoon = 5 ml spoon.
1 tablespoon = 15 ml spoon.

CONTENTS

INTRODUCTION

Cake decorating is fun, satisfying and rewarding, and with *The Book of Cake Decorating* you will be able to make any cake look really special, even if you are a novice.

Fully illustrated throughout with clear step-by-step instructions and photographs, *The Book of Cake Decorating* will teach and inspire you to create attractive and impressive cakes. The front section guides you through everything you need to know. There is advice on the equipment that is needed, tested basic recipes, how to master important techniques, from covering cakes through all the stages of piping, to making decorations to fit onto a cake for a really professional finish.

The second section includes explicit details on how to make a wide selection of imaginative, effective examples of decorated cakes at all levels of intricacy. There are both classic and novel ideas for many different occasions, such as a stunning cake to mark a Silver Wedding, a Golfer's Cake for a golf fanatic; a delightful Teddy Bear that will make any toddler's eyes light up; a Calculator cake for a teenager, and a pretty peach-coloured cake for a girl.

Stencils to help you with lettering and scroll work are also included at the back of this book.

EQUIPMENT

Simple cake decorating requires only everyday kitchen equipment, but more complicated designs require progressively a greater range of more specialist items. Buy the best that you can afford, especially if you expect to do quite a lot of icing.

Cakeboards – A wide selection of different sizes and shapes is available to match the sizes and shapes of cake tins. As a general guide, use a cake board that is 5 cm (2 in) larger than the cake. For very large cakes, use a board that is 7.5 cm (3 in) larger.

Cake tins – As well as the standard round and square tins, there is an interesting range of other shapes, such as hearts, octagonal shapes, numbers, petals etc.

Cocktail sticks – For adding colourings to icing, in modelling and helping to frill paste or icing.

Colourings – Always make sure the colouring is edible.
Liquid colourings are readily available but best used for pastel shades as they make icing too soft when used in large amounts. Add to the icing gradually using the point of a cocktail stick.
Paste colours are also readily available in a wide range of colours, and are economical as they are concentrated. They are most suitable for royal icing and sugarpaste.
Petal dust for colouring frills, filigree and lace work as well as flowers, available both plain and with a glitter effect.
Sugarcraft pens are used for writing and marking outlines.

Crimpers – Are a quick and versatile way of decorating surfaces covered by sugarpaste or almond paste. They come in a range of different effects, such as single scallop, diamonds, chevron, heart, holly. Simple ones can be used to create designs. Dip the ends in cornflour (cornstarch) during use to prevent sticking.

Craftknife, or scriber – For marking patterns on cakes.

Cutters – Cocktail or aspic, flower, biscuit (cookie) and pastry cutters.

Garrett frill cutter – An all in one cutter specially designed to cut out frills.

Glass-headed pins or icing nails – For piped flowers.

Greaseproof (waxed) paper – For making piping (pastry) bags and templates.

Icing ruler – A metal straight-edge for ensuring a perfectly flat royal iced surface.

Paint brushes – Fine artists' brushes; sable are best.

Palette knives – For spreading icings and mixing colours into royal icing.

Paring knife – For trimming sugarpaste and royal-iced cakes.

Piping nozzles (tubes) – A wide range is available, each one being referred to by a number. Unfortunately, manufacturers do not all use the same numbering system, so check with the applicable chart before buying. Nickel nozzles (tubes) are more expensive, but give more accurate and defined decorations than plastic. Nozzles (tubes) with a screw-thread fit, commercial piping (pastry) bags and pumps that are fitted with a screw collar, are useful in allowing the nozzle (tube) to be changed whilst the bag or pump is filled with icing.

Scrapers – For applying and smoothing royal icing on the sides of cakes.

Scissors – Large scissors for cutting greaseproof (waxed) paper, small, sharp, fine straight-bladed ones, such as those used for embroidery for moulded flowers.

Smoothers – Essential for perfectly-smooth sugarpaste and almond pasted cakes.

Spacers – Useful for ensuring a uniform thickness when rolling out almond paste or sugarpaste.

Turntable – Invaluable if cakes are royal iced frequently; an upturned plate will do for an occasional cake. A turntable should be heavy and strong and, preferably, tilt to facilitate decorating the sides of cakes.

Waxed paper and cellophane – For run-outs and piped flowers.

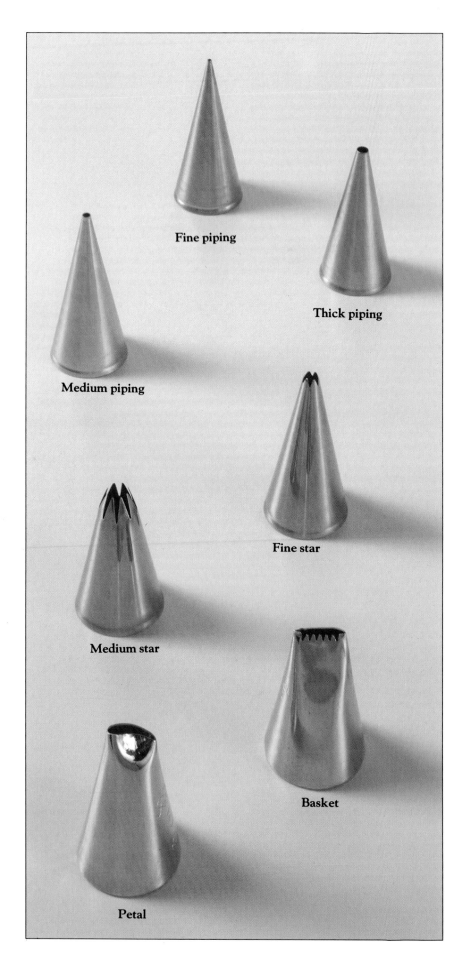

Fine piping

Thick piping

Medium piping

Fine star

Medium star

Basket

Petal

—————— RICH FRUIT CAKE ——————

440 g (14 oz/3 cups) currants
200 g (7 oz/1^1/4 cups) sultanas
200 g (7 oz/1^1/4 cups) raisins
55 g (2 oz/^{1}/2 cup) flaked almonds
55 g (2 oz/^{1}/3 cup) candied mixed peel
85 g (3 oz/^{1}/2 cup) glacé cherries, chopped
grated rind and juice of 1 lemon
3 tablespoons sherry
250 g (8 oz/1 cup) butter
200 g (7 oz/1^1/3 cups) soft brown sugar
3 eggs, beaten
200 g (7 oz/1^3/4 cups) plain (all-purpose) flour
1 teaspoon mixed spice

Preheat the oven to 135C (275F/Gas 1).

Line a 20 cm (8 in) round cake tin with a double thickness of greased greaseproof (waxed) paper, extending the paper above the sides. Place tin on a treble thickness of greaseproof (waxed) paper on a baking sheet. In a bowl, mix dried fruits, almonds, mixed peel, glacé cherries, lemon rind, juice and sherry. In another bowl beat butter and sugar until soft, then beat in eggs. Using a spoon, stir in dried fruit mixture. Sift flour and spice over surface and mix in until evenly combined. Spoon into tin. Level top with back of spoon and form a depression in the centre.

Bake for 3¼ – 3½ hours, until a skewer inserted in centre comes out clean. Leave to cool, then remove, remove lining paper and leave the cake with the top uppermost on a wire rack to cool completely.

Makes one 20 cm (8 in) round cake; or one 20 cm (8 in) hexagonal cake, or one 18 cm (7 in) square cake; or one 20 cm (8 in) heart-shaped cake.

Note: For quantities for other sizes see page 116

— VICTORIA SANDWICH CAKE —

185 g (6 oz/³/₄ cup) butter
185 g (6 oz/1 cup) caster (superfine) sugar
3 eggs, beaten
185 g (6 oz/1¹/₂ cups) plain (all-purpose) flour,
   sifted
few drops of vanilla essence, if desired

Preheat the oven to 190C (375F/Gas 5). Grease two 20 cm (8 in) sandwich tins. In a bowl, using a wooden spoon, beat the butter and sugar together until light and fluffy. Gradually beat in the eggs, beating well after each addition.

Using a wooden spoon, gradually and lightly fold in the flour until just evenly combined; add the vanilla essence near the end of the mixing, if desired. Divide between the sandwich tins and bake for 20 – 25 minutes until golden and the centre of each cake feels springy when lightly pressed. Invert one cake onto a wire rack; invert the other onto your hand then invert onto the wire rack so the right side is uppermost Leave to cool completely.

Makes two 20 cm (8 in) round sandwich cakes.

Variation: To make a Chocolate cake, replace 15 g (½ oz) of the flour with 15 g (½ oz) sifted cocoa powder.

Note: This mixture is also sufficient to make one 20 cm (8 in) deep round cake; OR one shallow 20 cm (8 in) square cake; OR an 18 cm (7 in) square cake; OR a shallow 25 x 20 cm (8 x 10 in) oblong cake.

— WHISKED SPONGE CAKE —

3 eggs
85 g (3 oz/^{1}/$_3$ cup) caster (superfine) sugar
85 g (3 oz/^{3}/$_4$ cup) plain (all-purpose) flour
pinch of salt

Preheat the oven to 190C (375F/Gas 5). Grease two 20 cm (8 in) sandwich tins. Put the eggs and sugar into a bowl, place over a saucepan of hot water then whisk together until very thick and light and the surface will support the weight of a trail of mixture left by the whisk. Remove the bowl from the heat. Sieve half of the flour and the salt over the mixture.

Using a metal spoon and a figure of eight movement, lightly fold in until just evenly combined. Repeat with the remaining flour. Divide between the cake tins and bake in the oven for 10-12 minutes until the top springs back when lightly pressed with the fingertips and has shrunk slightly from the sides of the tins. Invert one cake onto a wire rack; invert the other onto your hand then invert onto the wire rack so the right side is uppermost. Leave to cool completely.

Makes two 20 cm (8 in) round sandwich cakes.

Variation: To make a Chocolate cake, replace 15 g (½ oz) of the flour with 15 g (½ oz) sifted cocoa powder.

Note: This mixture is also sufficient to make one 20 cm (8 in) deep round cake; OR one shallow 20 cm (8 in) square cake; OR an 18 cm (7 in) square cake; OR a shallow 25 x 20 cm (8 x 10 in) oblong cake.

BUTTERCREAM

155 g (5 oz/^{2}/3 cup) unsalted butter, softened
200 g (7 oz/1^1/4 cups) icing (confectioner's)
  sugar, sifted
1 tablespoon lemon juice

In a bowl, using a wooden spoon, beat the
butter until soft.

Gradually beat in the sugar and lemon
juice to give a fairly firm but spreadable
consistency. Beat until the buttercream is
light and fluffy.

Use half of the buttercream to sandwich
the cakes together.

Using a palette knife, spread the remaining buttercream evenly over the cake.

To make a decorative effect, use a serrated
scraper.

Makes 375 g (12 oz).

ALMOND PASTE

500 g (1 lb/4½ cups) ground almonds
200 g (7 oz/2 cups) icing (confectioner's) sugar, sifted
200 g (7 oz/1 cup) caster (superfine) sugar
4 egg yolks
½ teaspoon almond essence
1 teaspoon lemon juice
4 tablespoons apricot jam, boiled, sieved and cooled
20 cm (8 in) square cake

In a bowl, stir together the ground almonds and both the sugars.

In a small bowl, stir together the egg yolks with the almond essence and lemon juice. Stir into the ground almond mixture and mix to a firm paste. Keep covered to prevent drying out. To cover a cake to be covered with Quick Sugarpaste, pack almond paste around the bottom of the cake to fill in gaps.

On a surface lightly dusted with icing (confectioner's) sugar, roll out the almond paste until it is large enough to completely cover the top and sides of the cake; use a length of string as a measure. Brush the cake with the apricot jam.

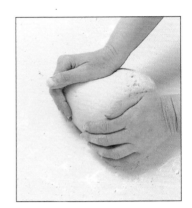

Using a rolling pin, carefully lift the almond paste on the back of your hands and transfer to the cake, placing the paste centrally.

Gently mould the almond paste around the cake and trim away the excess. Leave to dry for 24 hours.

Makes 1 kg (2 lb) almond paste

Note: For other quantities and yields, see page 117.

Store almond paste in a plastic bag in the refrigerator; it will keep for 2-3 days.

ALMOND PASTE FOR ROYAL ICING

Almond Paste, see page 16
icing (confectioner's) sugar for dusting
apricot jam, boiled, sieved and cooled
Rich Fruit Cake, see page 11

Place cake on a cake board and pack almond paste around bottom to fill in the gaps. Divide off almost half of the almond paste and reserve. Divide remainder into 4 (see Note). On a surface dusted with icing (confectioner's) sugar, evenly roll out each piece to a strip 5 mm (¼ in) thick, the depth and length of the sides of the cake; use a length of string as a measure.

Trim the edges; reserve the trimmings. Brush the sides of cake with the apricot jam. Carefully lift the strips to the sides and press gently in place. Add the trimmings to the reserved almond paste then roll out to a circle large enough to cover the top of the cake. Trim the edges. Brush the top of the cake with apricot jam. Using a rolling pin, carefully lift the almond paste, and place centrally on the cake. Press into place.

Using a small palette knife, smooth the joins. Polish the sides and top with a smoother, or palms of hands dusted with icing (confectioner's) sugar. Leave in a warm, dry place for at least 24 hours before icing.

Note: If covering a round cake, divide in half and roll out each piece long enough to go half way around the cake.

— SEVEN-MINUTE FROSTING —

1 egg white
155 g (5 oz) caster (superfine) sugar
pinch of salt
2 tablespoons water
pinch cream of tartar
20 cm (8 in) round Victoria Sandwich Cake, see
    page 12, or Whisked Sponge Cake, see
    page 13
Crystallised Flowers, see page 28

In a bowl, mix together lightly the egg white, sugar, salt water and cream of tartar. Place over a saucepan of gently simmering water and whisk hard until the mixture is very thick and stands in stiff peaks.

Remove bowl from the heat, immediately pour the frosting over the cake and spread to cover evenly.

Decorate with crystallised flowers and leave to set.

Makes one 20 cm (8 in) round cake.

—— QUICK SUGARPASTE ——

500 g (1 lb/4 cups) icing (confectioner's) sugar
1 egg white
2 tablespoons glucose syrup
icing (confectioner's) sugar for dusting
sherry or cooled boiled water to moisten

Sift the icing (confectioner's) sugar into a bowl. Using a wooden spoon, mix in the egg white and glucose syrup, then knead well.

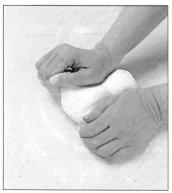

Turn onto a work surface dusted with icing (confectioner's) sugar and knead until smooth and pliable. Knead in a few drops of water if the icing is too firm.

Add a little food colouring and knead again until an even coloured paste is attained.

Roll out the sugarpaste until it is large enough to completely cover the top and sides of the cake; use a length of string as a measure. Moisten the surface of the almond paste by lightly brushing with sherry or cooled boiled water. Using a rolling pin, lift the sugarpaste onto the cake, placing it centrally, gently mould the sugarpaste around the cake. Pierce any air bubbles with a pin.

Place the paste centrally on the cake. Brush off excess icing (confectioner's) sugar. With hands well dusted with icing (confectioner's) sugar, or using a smoother, smooth the icing over the top and then down the sides of the cake, easing out any trapped air, and pressing the paste in place.

Still with sugar-dusted hands or a smoother, rub the surface of the cake in circular movements to make it smooth and shiny. Using a knife, trim surplus paste from the base.

Makes 625 g (1¼ lb) sugarpaste, to cover a 18 cm (7 in) square cake, or a 20 cm (8 in) round cake.

Note: Keep Quick Sugarpaste in a well-sealed plastic bag until immediately before using. For other quantities and yields see page 117.

ROYAL-ICED CAKE

20 cm (8 in) round or 18 cm (7 in) square cake
covered with Almond Paste, see page 18

Icing:
3 egg whites
750 g (1½ lb/4½ cups) icing (confectioner's)
sugar, sifted
1½ teaspoons glycerine

For the icing, in a bowl, using a fork, lightly whisk the egg whites. Stir in sufficient icing (confectioner's) sugar to make a consistency of unwhipped double (thick) cream.

Using a wooden spoon, beat in small amounts of icing (confectioner's) sugar until the mixture is very white and stiff peaks will form. Beat in the glycerine. Cover with a damp cloth. Spoon some icing onto the cake then, using a palette knife, smooth it to the edges.

In one movement, draw an icing ruler or long palette knife held at a 45 degree angle, across the top of the cake; maintain an even firm pressure. Remove surplus icing. Leave to dry for 12 hours.

Place on an upturned plate, or icing turn-table. Spread a thin but covering layer of icing round the sides of the cake.

Holding an icing scraper or palette knife at a 45 degree angle to the cake, place both hands at the back of the cake. Rotate the cake, bringing both hands to the front. Remove the scraper or knife at an angle and fairly quickly so the join is hardly visible. Using a palette knife remove any excess icing from the top.

Leave to dry for 12 hours. Repeat twice or even 3 more times until the finish is perfect. Leave for 24 hours before decorating.

Makes 825 g (1³/₄ lb) icing.

Note: For other quantities and yields, see page 117.

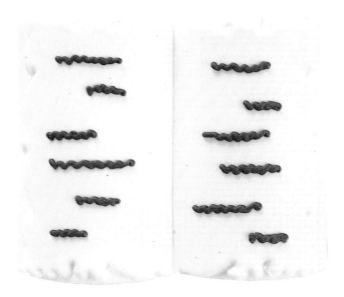

——— MOULDING ICING ———

1 tablespoon liquid glucose
2 tablespoons water
1 teaspoon powdered gelatine
375 g (12 oz/3 cups) icing (confectioner's) sugar, sifted

Put the liquid glucose and water into a bowl, sprinkle over the gelatine and leave to soak for 5 minutes. Place the bowl over a saucepan of hot water until the gelatine has dissolved.

Using a wooden spoon, gradually stir the icing (confectioner's) sugar into the gelatine mixture.

Turn onto a work surface lightly dusted with icing (confectioner's) sugar and knead until smooth and pliable. Wrap in a plastic bag and place in an airtight container.

To make plaques, roll out the moulding icing very thinly and cut out shapes using cutters or cardboard templates.

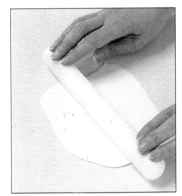

Leave the plaques on a flat surface to dry completely before using.

To make a book, roll out moulding icing very thinly and cut out a rectangle. Place over a double curved surface. Cut a smaller rectangle with a fancy edge and attach to the first rectangle. Allow to dry completely before piping the inscription.

Makes 440 g (14 oz).

SUGAR CRYSTAL DECORATIONS

410 g (13 oz) caster (superfine) sugar
3-4 teaspoons water
edible blue, red, green and yellow liquid food
    colourings

Place the sugar in a bowl. Using a fork, gradually stir in sufficient cold water until the sugar resembles damp sand. Divide between 5 bowls. Tint the sugar in one bowl pale blue, in another pink, another pale green and one pale yellow; leave 1 white. To make small shapes, use plastic decoration moulds, fill one shape with sugar at a time, pressing it in firmly.

To insert ribbon for hanging the decorations, add a loop of ribbon when the mould is half-filled, then complete the filling and press well down. Alternatively, use a skewer to make a hole when the sugar is almost set. Fill the remaining moulds in the same way. Place a flat tray over the moulds and invert. Lift off the moulds and leave the sugar shapes in a warm, dry place to set.

To make bells firmly pack sugar into the mould and invert on to a tray. Leave until the sugar has set on the outside to form a crust. Return the sugar shape to the mould and scoop out the sugar in the centre, leaving a hollow shape. Using a skewer, carefully pierce holes for ribbons, if desired. Remove the moulds and leave the sugar shapes to harden.

Makes about 25 decorations.

—— CHOCOLATE SHAPES ——

55 g (2 oz) plain (dark) chocolate

Place the chocolate in a bowl, and put over a saucepan of hot water. Leave until melted, stirring occasionally, until smooth. Pour onto a flat surface covered with greaseproof or waxed paper, and spread in an even, thin layer. Leave until it is just firm.

Cut out shapes using petits fours or aspic cutters, or cut squares or triangles with a sharp knife.

For piping, thicken the melted chocolate by carefully adding 1 or 2 drops of glycerine. Place in a greaseproof (waxed) paper piping (pastry) bag without the end cut off, or a nozzle (tube) fitted Cut the tip off the bag to make a small hole, and pipe filigree patterns.

— CRYSTALLISED FLOWERS —

1 egg white, lightly beaten
completely, dry, perfect fresh flowers, such as
    apple blossom, primroses, or petals from
    fragrant roses, or violets
caster (superfine) sugar, for coating

Hold the flower or petal carefully by the stem, and, using an artist's paintbrush, carefully brush the flowers or petals with a light, even coating of egg white, taking care to reach right inside the petals.

Sprinkle with caster (superfine) sugar to coat thoroughly and evenly; shake off excess Place on a wire rack or non-stick silicone paper and leave to dry then coat again. Shake off any excess sugar. Keep in an airtight container in a cool place for up to 2 days.

Makes 6 or more crystallised flowers.

Note: For longer term storage, replace the egg white with 125 ml (4 fl oz/½ cup) triple strength rose water shaken with 55 g (2 oz) gum arabic crystals in a screwtop jar; leave in the refrigerator for 12 – 24 hours, giving an occasional shake.

CRIMPING

cake covered in Almond Paste, see page 17,
or Quick Sugarpaste, see page 21
icing (confectioner's) sugar

Hold the crimpers with the teeth approximately 5 mm (¼ in) apart. Place on the surface of the cake and gently squeeze the the crimper closed. Release the pressure and remove the crimper. Dip the ends of the crimper in icing (confectioner's) sugar to prevent sticking.

Crimpers can be used to make decorative patterns.

Crimpers can also be used to form a decoration on the sides of the cake.

MOULDED FRUITS

Almond Paste, see page 16, in various suitable colours eg orange, pale green, red, yellow caster (superfine) sugar for dusting

Break off small pieces of Almond Paste. On a surface lightly dusted with caster (superfine) sugar form into miniature fruit shapes.

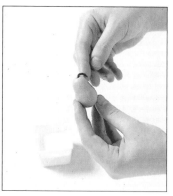

Form small pieces of brown almond paste as stalks and calyx.

Using a fine artist's paintbrush, paint the fruit with liquid food colouring to give a more realistic finish.

Note: Roll strawberries in caster (superfine) sugar; roll oranges and lemons on a fine grater to give a rough surface.

— ALMOND PASTE CUT-OUTS —

edible green and red paste food colourings
Almond Paste, see page 16
icing (confectioner's) sugar for dusting

In a small bowl, knead green food colouring into some Almond Paste On a work surface dusted with icing (confectioner's) sugar, roll out to 3 mm (¹/₈ in) thick. Using small aspic, cocktail or petits fours cutters, or a knife, cut out shapes.

Colour the remaining almond paste red. Roll out. Using a sharp knife, cut out letters. Arrange on the cake.

Note: Cut-outs can be made in the same way from Quick Sugarpaste.

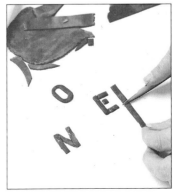

── MOULDED CARNATION ──

icing (confectioner's) sugar for dusting
Quick Sugarpaste, see page 20

On a surface lightly dusted with icing (confectioner's) sugar, roll out the Quick Sugarpaste very thinly. Using a fluted biscuit (cookie) cutter, or special carnation cutter, cut out a circle.

Using a cocktail stick as a small rolling pin, roll around the edge of one scallop until very fine and frilly. Repeat with the next scallop.

Using a little water, moisten the centre of the first scallop then place the second scallop on top. Use very small pieces of absorbent kitchen paper to prop up parts of the second scallop to prevent it becoming too flat. Repeat this procedure 5 or more times, stacking the scallops on top of each other, until the centre is drawn in so much that it is too small to take another 'petal'.

Cut one more petal and frill as above. Moisten the centre and fold it in half. Moisten again and fold into 3.

Moisten the inside of the flower and attach the folded petal. Arrange the petals with a cocktail stick and leave to dry.

Leave finished flowers to dry.

MOULDED ROSE

icing (confectioner's) sugar for dusting
Quick Sugarpaste, see page 20, or Almond
    Paste, see page 16

On a surface lightly dusted with icing
(confectioner's) sugar, mould a piece of
sugarpaste or almond paste about the size
of a walnut, into a cone.

From another piece of paste, form a small
pea-sized ball, place between two sheets of
plastic and press out until very thin.

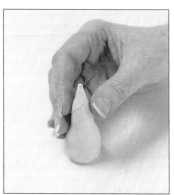

Remove the plastic, lightly moisten the
base of the disc of sugarpaste then wrap
around the cone to enclose it completely.

Make a waist in the covered cone to define the shape.

Form two more petals in the same way and place around the cone. Repeat, adding a third row of 3 petals, then a fourth row of 4 petals.

Trim the sugarpaste below the waist. Leave to dry.

SIMPLE PIPING

Royal Icing, see pages 22

To make a greaseproof (waxed) paper piping (pastry) bag, fold a rectangle of greaseproof (waxed) paper diagonally in half to make 2 equal triangles. Cut along the fold.

Fold the blunt end of the triangle over to form a cone; hold together. Bring the sharp end of the triangle over the cone.

Hold all the points together and adjust until the tip of the cone is very sharp; they will not line-up exactly. Fold the points inside the cone to hold the bag firmly. Snip off the end of the cone and insert the nozzle (tube) required.

Fill the icing bag to half to two-thirds full.
Fold the top of the bag over the icing.

To pipe simple letters, using a piping
(pastry) bag fitted with a medium writing nozzle (tube), holding the bag upright
slightly above the surface, pipe simple
letters.

To overpipe, use a piping (pastry) bag fitted
with a fine nozzle (tube) and filled with
icing of a contrasting colour, overpipe the
letters.

SIMPLE PIPING

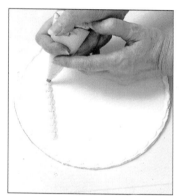

To pipe stars, using a piping (pastry) bag fitted with a star nozzle (tube), hold the bag at a 90 degree angle to the cake. Press on top of the icing in the bag until the star is the required size. Immediately release the pressure and pull the bag away. Repeat, making sure all the stars are the same size.

To pipe shells, using a piping (pastry) bag fitted with a star nozzle (tube), hold the bag at a 45 degree angle. Press on top of the icing in the bag until the shell is the required size. Immediately release the pressure and move the bag to one side, pushing the bag down as you do so.

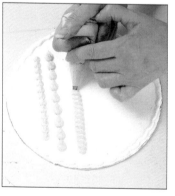

To pipe a rope, using a piping (pastry) bag fitted with a star or rope nozzle (tube), hold the bag at a 45 degree angle close to the surface of the cake. Press on the top of the icing in the bag until the icing is attached to the cake. Still squeezing at a constant pressure rotate the nozzle (tube) in a circular motion while slowly moving along the side of the cake.

To pipe an 'S' scroll, using a piping (pastry) bag fitted with a nozzle (tube) held at a 45 degree angle, gently squeeze on top of the icing in the bag maintaining a constant pressure rotating the nozzle (tube) and moving in a curved line.

To pipe a 'C' scroll, use the same nozzle (tube) and the same technique as forming an 'S' scroll, but rotate the nozzle (tube) in an anti-clockwise direction.

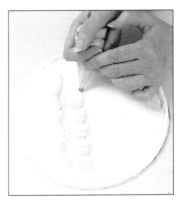

To overpipe, place a contrasting-coloured icing in a piping (pastry) bag fitted with a smaller nozzle (tube), holding the bag at a 45 degree angle, with the nozzle (tube) just above the scroll, follow its shape, using the same technique.

BASKET WEAVE

Royal Icing, see page 22, see Note

Using a piping (pastry) bag fitted with a plain nozzle (tube), pipe a straight line.

Using a piping (pastry) bag fitted with a basket weave nozzle (tube), pipe short lines over the straight line, leaving a space the width of the nozzle (tube) between each line.

Using the bag fitted with the plain nozzle (tube), pipe a second straight line along the end of the short lines. Using the bag fitted with the basket weave nozzle (tube), pipe a second set of short lines in the spaces between the first set. Continue until the required area is filled.

Note: Buttercream, see page 14, can also be used.

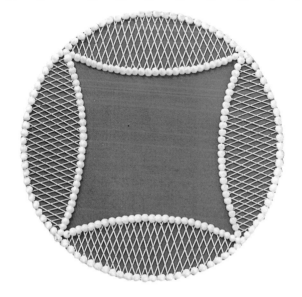

TRELLIS

Royal Icing, see page 22

Using a piping (pastry) bag filled with royal icing and fitted with a fine writing nozzle (tube), pipe a diagonal line across the centre of the area to be decorated. Working to one side of the line, pipe further lines parallel to the first until the area is filled.

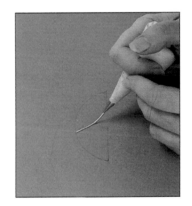

Pipe similar lines to the other side of the central line.

Rotate the cake a quarter turn, and repeat the process across the existing lines, from right to left.

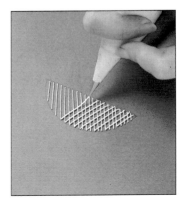

PIPED LEAVES

**Royal Icing, see page 22, or Buttercream,
   see page 14**

Make a greaseproof (waxed) paper piping
(pastry) bag, see page 36, but do not cut
off the point. Fill the bag with royal icing
or buttercream, and fold over the top of
the bag. Press the pointed end between
the thumb and finger, then, using small,
sharp scissors, trim one side of the point.

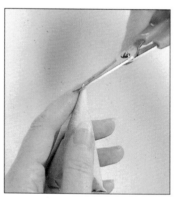

Trim the other side. Pipe leaves by gently
squeezing the top of the icing, and as the
icing comes out of the bag, raise it slightly.

When the leaf is the required size, reduce
the pressure and lift the bag away quickly
leaving a point. Make frilly leaves by
varying the pressure on the bag.

—————— PIPED ROSES ——————

Royal Icing made without glycerine, see page 22

Using a little royal icing without glycerine, attach a small square of waxed paper to an icing nail. Using a piping (pastry) bag fitted with a petal nozzle (tube), and keeping the nozzle (tube) upright, pipe a cone onto the waxed paper, keeping the thick end of the nozzle (tube) at the base.

Pipe further petals around the cone, always keeping the nozzle (tube) upright.

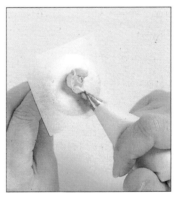

To make a larger rose, hold the nozzle (tube) and pipe another row of petals, keeping the thick end of the nozzle (tube) tucked in under the first row.

—— PIPED NARCISSUS ——

white Royal Icing made without glycerine, see page 22
edible yellow paste food colouring

Using a little royal icing without glycerine, attach a small square of waxed paper to an icing nail. Using a piping (pastry) bag fitted with a petal nozzle (tube), gently turning the nail as you work, pipe 6 petals in a circle, moving the nozzle (tube) out and in for each petal.

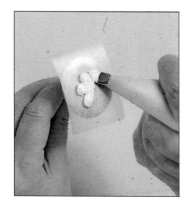

Using a slightly damp fine paintbrush, stroke along the centre of each petal to produce a slight point.

Colour some royal icing yellow and place in a piping bag fitted with a fine nozzle (tube) and pipe a spiral to form a trumpet shape.

───── PAINTED FLOWERS ─────

edible liquid food colourings

For complicated patterns, trace the design onto a greaseproof (waxed) paper then mark onto the cake using a craft knife or fine, sharp knife. Simple designs can be painted freehand. Pour a few drops of food colouring into a saucer. Using a fine paintbrush, paint in flower stems; do not overload the brush. Use light strokes, but build up the stems with successive strokes. Paint in the outline of the leaves, and fill in.

Wash the brush in clean water and dry thoroughly before changing colour. Paint in the outline of the flowers, then fill in, leaving a small circle in the centre free.

Leave to dry. Wash and dry the brush. Carefully paint in the centres.

COCOA PAINTING

Plaque, see page 25
1 teaspoon white vegetable fat
1-2 teaspoons cocoa powder

Trace the outline of the design onto greaseproof (waxed) paper. Using a craft knife, transfer the design onto the plaque.

Pour boiling water into a shallow dish and cover with a saucer. Put the vegetable fat on one side of the saucer and a teaspoon-ful of cocoa powder on the other. Allow the fat to melt. Using a fine paintbrush, mix a very small amount of cocoa with a little of the fat. Paint the palest areas of the design.

Gradually add more cocoa powder as needed for painting in darker areas. Use a strong mixture for the final details. Take care not to touch the picture as the colours will smudge.

EMBROIDERY USING A TEMPLATE

Royal Icing, see page 22

Using an embroidery pattern as a guide, trace the pattern onto greaseproof (waxed) paper. Place the greaseproof (waxed) paper on the cake in the position required.

Using a craft knife or fine, sharp knife, transfer the main details of the pattern onto the cake. Do not cut too deeply otherwise it will be difficult to cover the marks. A large pin can also be used, and is recommended for small details.

Lift off the template. Using a piping (pastry) bag filled with royal icing and fitted with a fine writing nozzle (tube), pipe over the marked lines. Additional details can be piped in freehand.

BRUSH EMBROIDERY

Royal Icing, see page 22

Trace the outline of a design onto greaseproof (waxed) paper. Place the tracing on a cake and transfer the design by cutting through the tracing with a sharp scalpel or knife.

With a piping (pastry) bag fitted with a fine writing nozzle (tube), pipe around the outline of the design, working on the background areas first and only working on a small area at a time. With a very slightly damp paintbrush and long smooth strokes brush the icing from the edge to the centre of the design, leaving a ridge of icing at the edge fading away towards the centre.

When all the shading is done add details with a fine tube.

——— RIBBON INSERTION ———

surface covered with Quick Sugarpaste, see page 20

Using a ribbon insertion tool or a small, sharp knife, make small cuts in evenly-spaced pairs in the sugarpaste where the ribbon insertion is desired.

Cut small lengths of ribbon slightly longer than the distance between the cuts.

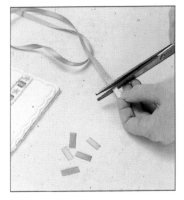

Push one end of the ribbon into one slit. Hold the piece of ribbon down and push the other end into the other slit. Finish off by piping with a very fine writing nozzle (tube).

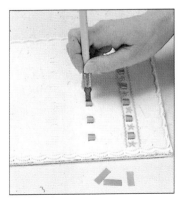

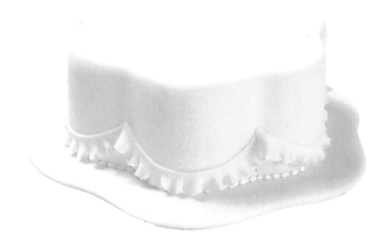

GARRETT FRILLS

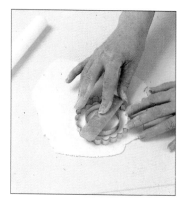

icing (confectioner's) sugar for dusting
Quick Sugarpaste, see page 20
cooled boiled water

On a surface lightly dusted with icing (confectioner's) sugar, roll out the sugarpaste to a very thin circle. Using a Garrett frill cutter or a 7.5 cm (3 in) fluted biscuit (cookie) cutter with a 5 cm (2 in) plain cutter placed inside, cut out a circle.

Using a cocktail stick as a miniature rolling pin, gently roll around the outside fluted edge until the edge is very fine and frilly. Keep moving the frill on the work surface to prevent sticking.

Cut through one side of the circle and open out to make a long frill. Attach to the cake with a little cooled boiled water.

Note: Quick Sugarpaste can be coloured to suit your cake.

STENCILLING

Royal Icing, see page 22

Place the stencil on the cake and hold in position to prevent it moving. Using a palette knife, spread a little royal icing over the stencil, making sure the pattern is completely covered.

Whilst the icing is still wet, carefully lift the stencil away from the cake, taking care not to smudge the icing. Leave to dry.

Multi-coloured stencils can be achieved by placing masking tape over areas of the stencil that are to be a different colour. Spread icing over. Remove the stencil and leave the icing to dry. Clean the stencil, mask off the areas already worked and uncover further areas. Continue as above.

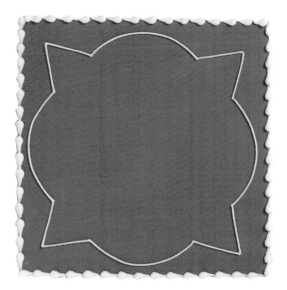

SIMPLE TOP TEMPLATE

cake covered with Royal Icing, page 22

Cut a square of greaseproof (waxed) paper exactly the same size as the top of the cake. Fold in half diagonally. Fold in half again, then in half once more.

Using a circular object, such as a saucer, as a guide, draw a curved pattern along the edge. Cut along the line.

Open out the template to place on the cake. Transfer the design to the cake by cutting through the paper using a craftknife or fine, sharp knife.

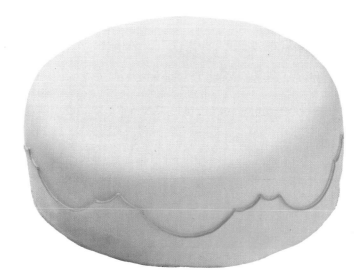

— SIMPLE SIDE TEMPLATE —

cake covered with Royal Icing, see page 22

Cut a strip of greaseproof (waxed) paper exactly the same length as the circumference of the cake, and the width of the height of the sides.

Fold the strip in half, then in half again and half once more. Using a circular object, such as a saucer, as a guide, mark a curved pattern along the middle of the strip. Cut along the line.

Open out the template to place on the cake. Transfer the design to the cake by cutting through the paper using a craftknife or fine, sharp knife.

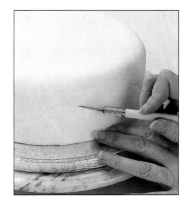

SIMPLE RUN-OUT

Royal Icing made without glycerine, see page 22

Trace the desired inscription or design onto strong greaseproof (waxed) paper and attach with short lengths of sticky tape to a piece of glass or other completely flat surface. Cover with clear film and hold in place with adhesive tape; make sure there are no wrinkles. Using a piping (pastry) bag filled with royal icing without glycerine and fitted with a fine writing nozzle (tube), pipe around the outline, making sure there are no gaps.

In a small bowl, add sufficient water to a little of the royal icing to give a creamy consistency which smooths out again after a slow count of seven when a knife is drawn across the surface. Fill into a greaseproof (waxed) paper piping (pastry) bag without a nozzle (tube) or hole. Cut a very small hole in the end of the piping (pastry) bag and fill in the outline; prick any bubbles while the icing is still very soft.

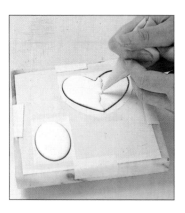

Leave to dry for at least 24 hours. Remove the clear film, and attach the run-out to the cake with a little royal icing. The completed plaque at the top of the page, shows the result which can be achieved by using this technique.

FEATHER-ICED CAKE

two 20 cm (8 in) round Chocolate Victoria
Sandwich Cakes, see page 12, or Whisked
Sponge Cakes, see page 13
500 g (1 lb) Chocolate Buttercream, see page 14
125 g (4 oz) plain (dark) chocolate, finely grated

Using 185 g (6 oz) buttercream, sandwich cakes together. Spread 125 g (4 oz) of the buttercream over the outside. To make glacé icing, put the icing (confectioner's) sugar into a small bowl, then stir in sufficient water to make a consistency that coats the back of the spoon. Transfer 2 tablespoonsful to another small bowl.

Stir 2 or 3 drops of cold water into the cocoa powder then stir into the small bowl. Place in a greaseproof (waxed) paper piping (pastry) bag without a hole in the end. Using a palette knife, spread the white glacé icing over the top of the cake, almost to the edge. Quickly cut just the very tip off the piping (pastry) bag to make a tiny hole then immediately pipe onto the cake in a continuous spiral, starting at the centre.

While the icing is still wet, draw a fine skewer or cocktail stick across the chocolate lines, from the centre to the outside. Press the chocolate onto the sides of the cake. Spoon the remaining chocolate buttercream into a piping (pastry) bag fitted with a medium star nozzle (tube), pipe swirls around the top edge of the cake.

Makes one 20 cm (8 in) round cake.

——— SIMPLE EASTER CAKE ———

20 cm (8 in) round Rich Fruit Cake, see page 11
3 tablespoons apricot jam, boiled, sieved and
    cooled
375 g (12 oz) Almond Paste, see page 16
125 g (4 oz) Royal Icing, see page 22

Using a large sharp knife, trim the top of the cake so that it is completely flat. Brush with the apricot jam. On a surface lightly dusted with icing (confectioner's) sugar, roll out 250 g (8 oz) of the almond paste to a 20 cm (8 in) circle. Place on top of the cake. Pinch around the edge to form a slight rim.

Add a few drops of cooled boiled water to the royal icing to make a consistency that spreads easily. Place in the centre of the almond paste, and use a palette knife to spread to the edge; take care that it does not flow over the edge. Leave to dry.

Divide the remaining almond paste into eleven evenly-sized balls. Place on a baking sheet and place under a hot grill for a few minutes until the tops are golden brown. Allow to cool. Place around the top edge of the cake. Place a wide, 65 cm (26 in) long gold ribbon around the cake and secure with a short length of clear adhesive tape.

Makes one 20 cm (8 in) cake.

SPEEDWAY

two 20 cm (8 in) square Victoria Sandwich
  Cakes, see page 12, or Whisked Sponge Cakes,
  see page 13
250 g (8 oz) Buttercream, see page 14
250 g (8 oz) Quick Sugarpaste, see page 20
375 g (12 oz) Royal Icing, see page 22
edible black and green paste food colourings
rice paper

Place the cakes side by side on a large
cakeboard. Using a sharp knife, cut to an
irregular shape. Cover the cakes with buttercream.

Knead a little black colouring into the
Quick Sugarpaste to colour it grey.
On a surface lightly dusted with icing
(confectioner's) sugar, roll out thinly to a
rectangle large enough to cover the top of
the cake. Place on the cake and, using a
small sharp knife, trim to shape of the
cake. Press lightly in position. Using a
skewer or back of a sharp knife, mark the
position of the 'islands'.

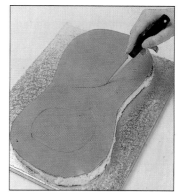

Colour the royal icing pale green. Place in
a piping (pastry) bag fitted with a medium
star nozzle (tube) and pipe stars in the islands and around the sides of the cake.
Cut out squares and triangles from rice
paper to resemble marker flags and the
finishing line. Using a little royal icing, attach to wooden cocktail sticks. Place on
the cake.

*Makes one approximately 38 cm (15 in) long
cake.*

─── RAINBOW CAKE ───

one 25 cm (10 in) round Victoria Sandwich
    Cake, see page 12, or Whisked Sponge
    Cake, see page 13
185 g (6 oz) Buttercream, see page 14
1 kg (2 lb 2 oz) Royal Icing, see page 22
edible blue, red, orange, yellow, green indigo
    and violet paste food colourings
55 g (2 oz) Quick Sugarpaste, see page 20
icing (confectioner's) sugar for dusting

Cut the cake into 2 semi-circles, then
sandwich together using two-thirds of the
buttercream. Spread the remaining buttercream over the cake.

On the top of the cake, mark a wavy line
about 1.25 cm (½ in) from the cut edge.
Partially mix a little blue colouring into
2 tablespoonsful of the royal icing and
spread in the centre of the cake, overlapping the marked line slightly.

Colour 125 g (4 oz) of the royal icing red, 125 g (4 oz) orange, 85 g (3 oz) yellow, 85 g (3 oz) green and 4 tablespoonsful each blue, indigo and violet. Using a piping (pastry) bag fitted with a medium star nozzle (tube) throughout, pipe 2 rows of stars of each colour, starting from the outside edge of the cake with red icing, then orange, yellow, green, blue, indigo and violet; the last 2 rows should overlap the blue 'sky' in the centre.

Colour 185 g (6 oz) of the royal icing blue, and pipe stars around the curved side of the cake to correspond with the stars in the red band at the top edge, and represent the sky.

Colour the remaining icing pale green and pipe stars in the area below the wavy line to represent grass.

On a surface lightly dusted with icing (confectioner's) sugar, roll out the Quick Sugarpaste. Cut out tree shapes. Place on the 'sky-line' on the cake.

Makes one 25 cm (10 in) cake.

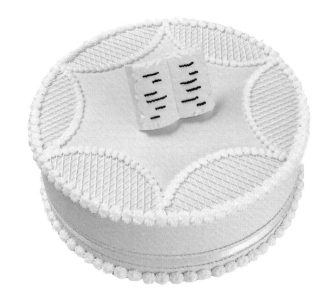

——————— TRELLIS CAKE ———————

One 20 cm (8 in) round Rich Fruit Cake, see
   page 11
4 tablespoons apricot jam, boiled, sieved and
   cooled
750 g (1 ½ lb) Almond Paste, see page 16
1 kg (2 lb) Royal Icing, see page 22

Cover the cake with Almond Paste, see
page 16. Colour 825 g (1 ³/₄ lb) royal icing
pale peach and cover the cake, see page
22. Divide the top edge of the cake into
six. Using a saucer or other suitable size
object as a guide, mark a curve between
each division using a sharp knife.

Fill a piping (pastry) bag fitted with a fine
writing nozzle (tube) with 4 tablespoons
white royal icing. Start piping the trellis design, see page 41, keeping the lines
straight and evenly spaced.

Continue piping the trellis lines in the opposite direction.

Place the remaining royal icing in a bag fitted with a fine star tube. Pipe small stars round the inner curves of the trellis to neaten the edge.

Continue piping stars round the top edge and round the base of the cake.

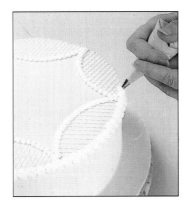

Using royal icing, attach a band of ribbon round the cake. Place an ornament in position if desired.

Makes one 20 cm (8 in) round cake.

CLOCK

two 23 cm (8 in) round Victoria Sandwich
   Cakes, see page 12, or Whisked Sponge
   Cakes, see page 13
250 g (8 oz) Buttercream, see page 14
icing (confectioner's) sugar for dusting
750 g (1½ lb) Quick Sugarpaste, see page 20
edible yellow and brown paste food colourings
85 g (3 oz) Royal Icing, see page 22
cooled boiled water

Sandwich cakes together with half of the
buttercream, cover with the remaining
buttercream, see page 15. Knead a little
yellow food colouring into 185 g (6 oz) of
the Quick Sugarpaste to colour it cream.

On a surface lightly dusted with icing
(confectioner's) sugar, roll out to a 20 cm
(8 in) circle. Carefully transfer to the top
of the cake, placing it centrally; press
lightly in position. Knead brown food
colouring into 375 g (12 oz) Quick Sugarpaste to colour light brown. Roll out to a
strip the depth of the cake wide and 26
cm (24 in) long. Place around the cake
and press lightly in position. Colour the
royal icing brown. Place 2 tablespoonsful in a piping (pastry) bag fitted with a
medium writing nozzle (tube) and pipe the
numerals on the clock.

Pipe the hands to correspond to the
child's age. Place remaining brown royal
icing in a bag fitted with a medium star
nozzle (tube) and pipe a rope around top
edge of cake, see page 38. With remaining
white Sugarpaste, mould two domed
shapes to represent bells, a roll to form
the handle and two small balls for legs.
Leave to dry. Paint with edible silver food
colouring, if desired. Using cooled boiled
water, fix to the sides of the cake.

Makes one 23 cm (8 in) cake.

—— THANKSGIVING CAKE ——

25 x 20 cm (10 x 8 in) rectangular Rich Fruit
    Cake, see page 11
1 kg (2 lb) Almond Paste, see page 16
4 tablespoons apricot jam, boiled, sieved and
    cooled
1 kg (2 lb) Quick Sugarpaste, see page 20
edible yellow paste food colouring
icing (confectioner's) sugar for dusting
4 tablespoonsful Royal Icing, see page 22
Almond Paste Fruits, see page 30

Measure 5 cm (2 in) along the cake, from
from each corner and cut off the corners.
Cover the cake with Almond Paste, see
page 17. Knead a little yellow food
colouring into the sugarpaste to colour it
cream, then cover the cake, see page 20.
Whilst the sugarpaste is still soft, using a
crimper, crimp around the top and side
edges.   Using yellow food colouring,
colour the royal icing cream. Place in a
piping (pastry) bag fitted with a small star
nozzle (tube) and pipe shells around the
base of the cake.

Using a little royal icing, fix almond paste
fruits at the bottom corners. Continue to
attach fruits to the top of the cake.

Makes one 25 x 20 cm (10 x 8 in) cake.

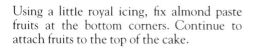

──── CALCULATOR ────

500 g (1 lb) Quick Sugarpaste, see page 20
edible yellow, black and red paste food colourings
icing (confectioner's) sugar for dusting
20 x 15 cm (8 x 6 in) Victoria Sandwich Cake,
see page 12, or Whisked Sponge cake, see
page 13
125 g (4 oz) Royal icing, see page 22
cooled boiled water

Divide off 55 g (2 oz) Quick Sugarpaste
and reserve in a plastic bag. Knead
yellow colouring into remainder to colour
cream, then use to cover Cake, see page
21. Using black colouring, colour 2
tablespoonsful royal icing grey.

Fill a piping (pastry) bag fitted with a
writing nozzle (tube). Pipe a line around
top of the cake and a straight line across
the cake two-thirds of the way up. Break
off a piece of reserved sugarpaste the size
of a walnut and reserve in the plastic bag.
Colour remaining sugarpaste grey. On a
surface dusted with icing (confectioner's)
sugar, roll out to a rectangle. Using a
knife, cut a strip 2 x 10 cm ($^3/_4$ x 4 in)
wide. Using cooled boiled water, attach to
the top of the cake. Cut remainder into 23
x 1 cm ($^3/_8$ in) squares, and a 2.5 x 1 cm (1
x $^3/_8$ in) strip and attach to the top of cake.
Using black and red colourings, colour
reserved sugarpaste deep red.

Roll out and cut to an 8 x 1.5 cm ($2^1/_2$ x
$^1/_2$ in) strip to fit top part of cake. Attach with cooled boiled water. Place 2
tablespoons Royal Icing in a bag fitted
with a fine writing nozzle (tube) and pipe
numbers and appropriate symbols on the
grey squares. Pipe an appropriate date on
the grey 'visual display panel'.

Makes one 20 x 15 cm (8 x 6 in) cake.

HEDGEHOG

**two 20 cm (8 in) round Victoria Sandwich
Cakes, see page 12, or Whisked Sponge
Cakes, see page 13**
500 g (1 lb) Chocolate Buttercream, see page 14
155 g (5 oz) Royal Icing, see page 22
edible black and green paste food colourings

Slice each cake in half to make 4
semi-circles. Using a quarter of the buttercream, sandwich the layers together.
Stand the cake on a cake board, cut edge
down.

Using a sharp knife, make the back of
the hedgehog by trimming the cake to a
rounded shape. Gather some of the trimmings together and form into a shape
for the nose. Spread the remaining buttercream over the cake. Mark the spines
with a fork.

Colour 2 tablespoonsful of the royal icing
black, place in a piping (pastry) bag fitted
with a thick writing nozzle (tube) and pipe
in the eyes and nose. Colour the remaining icing green. Spread roughly on the
board to represent grass.

Makes one 20 cm (8 in) long cake.

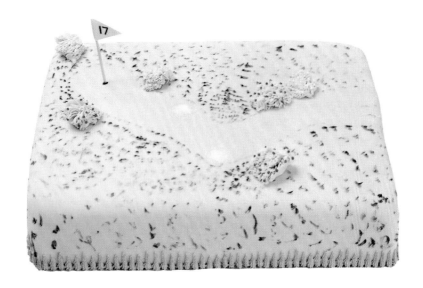

GOLFER'S CAKE

two 20 cm (8 in) square Victoria Sandwich Cakes,
 see page 12, or Whisked Sponge Cakes, see
 page 13
250 g (8 oz) Buttercream, see page 14
edible green paste food colourings
500 g (1 lb) Quick Sugarpaste, see page 20
icing (confectioner's) sugar for dusting

Decoration:
edible green liquid food colouring
edible green, yellow and black paste food
 colourings
125 g (4 oz) Quick Sugarpaste, see page 20
185 g (6 oz) Royal Icing, see page 22
rice paper
30 g (2 tablespoons) caster (superfine) sugar

Using half of the buttercream, sandwich
the cakes together, then cover with the
remaining buttercream. Knead green
paste colouring into the Quick Sugarpaste
and use to cover the cake, see page 20.
Using green liquid food colouring and a
fine paintbrush, stipple over the cake to
create the grass, leaving an area across the
centre to represent the fairway, and
making it wider at the end near the
'green'.

Knead green paste colouring into the Quick Sugarpaste. To make the bushes, push through a sieve, using the back of a spoon. When the strands on the back of the sieve are large enough, using a knife, carefully scrape them from the sieve. Attach to the cake using a little royal icing.

Place the sugar in a basin, add a very small amount of yellow food colouring and mix together with the fingertips until the sugar is yellow.

Moisten 2 small areas of the fairway and sprinkle with the yellow sugar to represent bunkers. Colour 2 tablespoonsful royal icing red, place in a piping (pastry) bag fitted with a fine writing nozzle (tube) and pipe very small dots over the bushes. Colour another 2 tablespoonsful icing yellow, place in a bag fitted with a fine writing nozzle (tube) and pipe some more very small dots over the bushes.

Use liquid food colouring, paint a very small dot in the centre of the 'green'. Attach a small triangle of rice paper to a cocktail stick and paint a number on it. Colour 125 g (4 oz) of the royal icing green, place in a bag fitted with a medium star nozzle (tube) and pipe elongated shells up the sides of the cake.

Makes one 20 cm (8 in) square cake.

PARCEL

250 g (8 oz) Buttercream, see page 14
two 20 cm (8 in) square Victoria Sandwich
    Cakes, see page 12, or Whisked Sponge
    Cakes, see page 13
500 g (1 lb) Quick Sugarpaste, see page 20
icing (confectioner's) sugar for dusting
edible pale blue paste food colouring

Decoration:
185 g (6 oz) Quick Sugarpaste, see page 20
edible blue food colour
icing (confectioner's) sugar for dusting
cooled boiled water
4 tablespoonsful Royal Icing, see page 22

Using half of the buttercream, sandwich cakes together. Spread with remaining buttercream. Knead a little blue colouring into Quick Sugarpaste to colour it pale blue, then use to cover cake, see page 20. For the decoration, break off 30 g (1 oz) Quick Sugarpaste, place in a plastic bag; reserve. Knead a little blue food colouring into remaining Sugarpaste to make deeper blue than cake.   Roll out thinly; cut into three strips approximately 2.5 x 30 cm (1 x 12 in); trim edges. Using a little of the royal icing, fix two strips to cake to form the ribbon.

Form remaining strip into a flat bow; fix to cake. Roll out reserved Sugarpaste, cut out a rectangle 5 x 2.5 cm (2 x 1 in). Using cooled boiled water, fix to cake.   Colour half royal icing deep blue and place in a piping (pastry) bag fitted with a fine writing nozzle (tube). Pipe a small scallop pattern round edge of the 'label'. Colour the royal icing pale blue; use to fill a piping (pastry) bag fitted with a star nozzle (tube), pipe stars around base of cake.

Makes one 20 cm (8 in) square cake.

EASTER BONNET

two 20 cm (8 in) round Victoria Sandwich
   Cakes, see page 12, or Whisked Sponge
   Cakes, see page 13
250 g (8 oz) Buttercream, see page 14

Decoration:
625 g (1 lb) Chocolate Buttercream, see page 14
approximately 8 Piped Narcissus, see page 44

Using half of the buttercream, sandwich
the cakes together. Cover with the
remaining buttercream.

Spoon the chocolate buttercream into a
piping (pastry) bag fitted with a basket
weave nozzle (tube) and pipe a basket
weave pattern over the sides of the cake,
see page 40. Using the back of a small,
sharp knife, mark the top of the cake into
sections, then fill with basket weave icing,
see page 40.

Pipe basket weave over the cake board to
make the hat brim. Attach the piped narcissus.

Makes one 20 cm (8 in) cake.

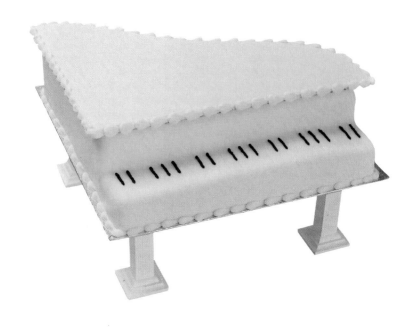

PIANO

two 23 cm (9 in) square Victoria Sandwich
    Cakes, see page 12, or Whisked Sponge
    Cake, see page 13
250 g (8 oz) Buttercream, see page 14
750 g (1½ lb) Quick Sugarpaste, see page 20
edible black paste food colouring
185 g (6 oz) Royal Icing, see page 22

Draw the top of the piano on a sheet of
greaseproof (waxed) paper. Use as a
template on 2 cake cards to make
piano shapes. Using half the Buttercream,
sandwich cakes together. Using a card
shape as a guide cut cake to a piano shape
making it slightly smaller than the card.

Cut away 5 cm (2 in) from the top of the
cake and one of the cards to represent the
keyboard.

Spread the remaining buttercream over the entire cake. Cover the cake with sugarpaste, see page 20, and place on the larger card. Place half of the royal icing in a piping bag fitted with a fine star nozzle (tube) and pipe shells around the base of the cake.

Gather up the sugarpaste trimmings then roll-out to cover the smaller card, and pipe shells around the edge using the same bag as before.

Using a cocktail stick mark divisions on the keyboard.

Colour the remaining royal icing black. Place in a piping (pastry) bag fitted with a fine writing nozzle (tube) and pipe in short, even, evenly spaced lines to represent the black keys. Place the piano lid on top of the cake and stand the whole cake on 3 cake pillars.

Makes approximately 23 cm (10 in) cake.

LOG CABIN

two 20 cm (8 in) square Chocolate Victoria
  Sandwich Cakes, see page 12, or Whisked
  Sponge Cakes, see page 13
750 g (1½ lb) Chocolate Buttercream, see
  page 14
250 g (8 oz) plain (dark) chocolate, broken
125 g (4 oz) Royal Icing, see page 22
edible green paste food colouring
125 g (4 oz) Quick Sugarpaste, see page 20

Cut the cakes in half to make 4 layers.
Using 125 g (4 oz) of the buttercream,
sandwich all the layers together. Mark a
line down the centre of the cake.

At an angle, cut through 1½ layers to
form the slope of the roof. Trim the edges
to give a neat finish. Using 125 g (4 oz)
buttercream, cover the cake. Melt chocolate and spread on greaseproof (waxed)
paper to approximately 23 cm (9 in)
square, see page 27. When just beginning
to set, mark into sixty 2.5 cm (1 in)
squares, one 7.5 x 4 cm (3 x 1½ in)
rectangle, and four 5 x 4 cm (2 x 1½ in)
rectangles.

Working across the cake from the bottom, and overlapping each row, place the squares on the roof. If necessary, use a little extra buttercream to help the 'tiles' to stick. Attach the larger rectangle of chocolate on one side of the cake for the door. Attach 2 smaller rectangles at the back and 2 at the front, for the windows.

Place the remaining buttercream in a piping (pastry) bag fitted with a medium star nozzle (tube) and pipe lines up the sides of the cabin to represent logs.

Then pipe a rope, see page 38, along the top edge of the cake.

Colour the royal icing green, then spread most of it over the board to represent grass. Knead green food colouring into the Quick Sugarpaste and mould into cones of varying sizes. Spread a little of the remaining green royal icing over each one and place on the grass at the front of the cabin.

Makes one 20 cm (8 in) square cake.

TOADSTOOL

two 15 cm (6 in) round Victoria Sandwich
    Cakes, see page 12, or Whisked Sponge
    Cakes, see page 13
one cake baked in a 1 litre (2 pint) ovenproof
    pudding bowl, see Note
375 g (12 oz) Buttercream, see page 14
icing (confectioner's) sugar for dusting
500 g (1 lb) Quick Sugarpaste
yellow, red, brown, green, pink edible paste
    food colourings
cooled boiled water
250 g (8 oz) Royal Icing, see page 22

Using 85 g (3 oz) of the buttercream,
sandwich the two round cakes together.
Spread another 85 g (3 oz) around the
sides. Knead a little yellow food colouring
into 250 g (8 oz) Quick Sugarpaste to
colour cream, then cover the cake, see
page 20.

Spread the remaining buttercream over the remaining cake. Knead red food colouring into 250 g (8 oz) Quick Sugarpaste; cover the cake. On a surface lightly dusted with icing (confectioner's) sugar, roll out 55 g (2 oz) white Quick Sugarpaste very thinly. Cut out about twelve 1.5 cm (½ in) diameter circles. Using a little cooled boiled water, attach to the red cake. Place on the cream cake.

Knead brown colouring into the remaining sugarpaste. On a surface lightly dusted with icing (confectioner's) sugar, roll out thinly. Using the point of a sharp knife, cut out door and window shapes. Using cooled boiled water attach to the sides of the cream cake.

Mix green colouring into 185 g (6 oz) of the royal icing. Place 4 tablespoonsful in piping (pastry) bag fitted with a medium writing nozzle (tube), and pipe vines up the sides of the cake. Knead red colour into 2 tablespoonsful royal icing and yellow colour into 2 tablespoonsful royal icing.

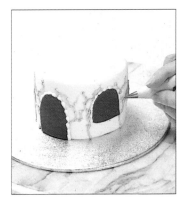

Using bags fitted with a fine writing nozzle (tube), pipe small bulbs to represent flowers. Roughly spread the remaining green icing over the cake board around the cake and pipe grass up the sides of the cake. Place the red cake on top of the cream cake.

Makes one 15 cm (6 in) cake.

Note: Use the recipe on page 12 and bake in an oven preheated to 170C (325F/Gas 3) for 1 hour.

— RABBITS-IN-BED —

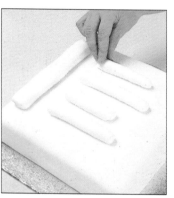

23 cm (9 in) square Victoria Sandwich Cake, see
  page 12, or Whisked Sponge Cake, see
  page 13
icing (confectioner's) sugar for dusting
500 g (1 lb) Quick Sugarpaste, see page 20

Decoration:
825 g (1 lb 10 oz) Quick Sugarpaste, see page 20
cooled boiled water
edible red and brown paste food colouring
250 g (8 oz) Royal Icing, see page 22

Cover the cake with Quick Sugarpaste,
see page 20. For the decoration, on
a surface lightly dusted with icing
(confectioner's) sugar, roll 55 g (2 oz)
Quick Sugarpaste into a 15 cm (6 in) long
roll, about 4 cm (1½ in) in diameter.
Slightly flatten to make a pillow. Using
cooled boiled water, position at the top of
the cake.

Divide off four approximately 55 g (2 oz) pieces of white sugarpaste and form each into a roll 5 – 7 cm (2 - 2½ in) long; place down the 'bed'. Place 115 g (4 oz) white royal icing in a bag fitted with a medium writing nozzle (tube) and pipe shells round the base of the cake.

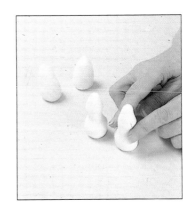

Divide off four 15 g (½ oz) pieces of sugarpaste and shape each into a cone; mould so that it is thinner in the middle. Cut through the thin part of each 'head' to make 'ears'. Bend the 'ears' of each 'head' to different angles and place on the pillow.

Using a little red food colouring, colour the remaining sugarpaste pink. Roll out to a thin square to cover the top of the cake. Trim the edges, carefully transfer to the cake, smoothing down between each 'body'. Place 2 tablespoonsful royal icing in a piping (pastry) bag fitted with a fine writing nozzle (tube), and pipe in the eyes.

Colour 2 tablespoonsful royal icing brown, place in a bag fitted with a fine writing nozzle (tube) and pipe in the pupils of the eyes. Colour the remaining royal icing deep pink. Place in a bag fitted with a fine writing nozzle (tube) and pipe an embroidery pattern on the quilt, freehand.

Makes one 23 cm (9 in) square cake.

TEDDY BEAR

two 20 cm (8 in) Victoria Sandwich Cakes, see
    page 12, or Whisked Sponge Cakes, see
    page 13
250 g (8 oz) Buttercream, see page 14
750 g (1 ½ lb) Royal Icing, see page 22
icing (confectioner's) sugar for dusting
185 g (6 oz) Quick Sugarpaste, see page 20
edible brown, yellow, pink, green and blue paste
    food colourings

Using half the buttercream, sandwich the
cakes together. Draw shape of bear on a
piece of greaseproof (waxed) paper. Cut
out shape and place centrally on top of
the cake. Using a sharp knife, cut around.

Using a palette knife, spread the remaining buttercream over the outside of the
cake. On a surface lightly dusted with
icing (confectioner's) sugar, roll out the
Quick Sugarpaste. Using a 9 cm (3½ in)
cutter, cut out 2 circles, to make the teddy
bear's stomach and face. Place on the
cake.

Reserve 4 tablespoonsful of the royal icing. Using brown and yellow colourings, colour the remainder golden brown, place in a piping (pastry) bag fitted with a medium star nozzle (tube) and pipe stars over all the buttercream-covered areas of the cake. Leave to dry overnight.

Using a fine paintbrush and brown and pink food colourings, paint the teddy bear's face.

Using yellow and green food colourings, paint a motif on the stomach.

Place half of the reserved icing in a bag fitted with a medium writing nozzle (tube) and pipe the inscription. Colour the remaining icing blue, place in a bag fitted with a fine writing nozzle (tube) and overpipe the inscription.

Makes one 25 x 20 cm (10 x 8 in) cake.

GIRL'S BIRTHDAY CAKE

20 cm (8 in) round Victoria Sandwich Cake, see page 12, or Whisked Sponge Cake, see page 13
250 g (8 oz) Buttercream, see page14
500 g (1 lb) Quick Sugarpaste, see page 20
icing (confectioner's) sugar for dusting
edible pink, and yellow paste food colourings
155 g (5 oz) Royal Icing, see page 22

Use half the Buttercream to sandwich the cakes together then spread the remainder over the cake. On a surface lightly dusted with icing (confectioner's) sugar, lightly knead pink food colouring into the sugarpaste to produce a marbled effect.

Cover the cake, see page 20. Knead the trimmings until evenly coloured; place in a plastic bag and reserve.

Mark the top of the cake into 6 equal sections, see page 53. Roll out the pink sugarpaste trimmings very thinly. From part of the trimmings, cut out 6 strips about 14 cm (5 in) long and 1 cm ($^{3}/_{8}$ in) wide, twist each strip twice then attach to the cake with a little royal icing to form garlands; keep the join as neat as possible.

From the remaining rolled out trimmings, using small flower cutters, cut out approximately 25 – 30 small flowers. Using a little royal icing, attach to the joins.

Colour 2 tablespoonsful of the remaining royal icing yellow, transfer to a bag fitted with a fine writing nozzle (tube) and pipe small dots in the centre of each flower.

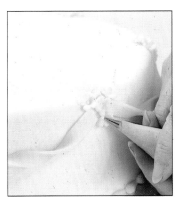

Colour the remaining royal icing pale pink and place in a bag fitted with a small star nozzle (tube) and pipe shells at the base of the cake.

Makes one 20 cm (8 in) round cake.

MOTHER'S DAY CAKE

20 cm (8 in) round Victoria Sandwich Cake, see
    page 12, or Whisked Sponge Cake, see page 13
250 g (8 oz) Chocolate Buttercream, see page 14
edible brown paste colouring
500 g (1 lb) Quick Sugarpaste, see page 20
icing (confectioner's) sugar for dusting
185 g (6 oz) Royal Icing, see page 22
6 Piped Roses, see page 43

Sandwich the cakes together using half
the chocolate buttercream. Spread the
remaining buttercream over the cake and
cover with the Quick Sugarpaste, see page
20, which has been coloured dark brown.

Draw a template, see page 52. Place on the
cake and cut through with a craft knife, or
very sharp, slim knife to mark the design
on the cake. Cut a strip of greaseproof
(waxed) paper 65 cm (26 in) long and 2.5
cm (1 in) wide. Use to make a line around
the side of the cake. Fold the strip in half
lengthwise and mark a second line below
the first, around the cake.

Place 2 tablespoonsful of the royal icing in a piping (pastry) bag fitted with a medium writing nozzle (tube) and pipe around the petal outline on the cake. Place 4 tablespoonsful of the royal icing in a bag fitted with a fine writing nozzle (tube) and pipe a continuous random line between the petal outline and the higher line on the side of the cake. Insert short lengths of narrow white ribbon between the marked lines on the side of the cake, see page 49.

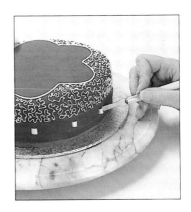

Using the bag fitted with the fine writing nozzle (tube), pipe an embroidery motif, see page 47, between each piece of ribbon. Then pipe a very small scalloped line along the marked lines above and below the ribbon insertion.

Using a little royal icing, attach piped roses in each scallop on top of the cake.

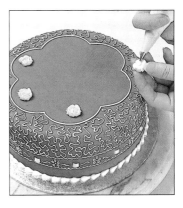

Colour 2 tablespoonsful of the icing green and place in a greaseproof (waxed) paper piping (pastry) bag without a hole at the point or a nozzle (tube). Cut the point to a 'V' shape, see page 42, and pipe leaves on either side of each rose, see page 42. Place the remaining white icing in a bag fitted with a fine star nozzle (tube) and pipe shells around the bottom of the cake.

Makes one 20 cm (8 in) round cake.

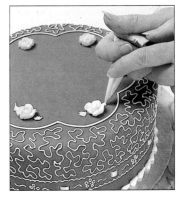

OVAL PEACH CAKE

20 cm (8 in) oval Rich Fruit Cake, see page 11
750 g (½ lb) Almond Paste, see page 16
4 tablespoons apricot jam, boiled sieved and
    cooled
icing (confectioner's) sugar for dusting
500 g (1 lb) Quick Sugarpaste, see page 20
edible peach and green paste food colourings
280 g (9 oz) Royal Icing, see page 22

Cover the cake with almond paste, see
page 17. Knead peach colouring into the
Quick Sugarpaste until lightly coloured
then use to cover the cake, see page 20.

For the decoration, colour 85 g (3 oz) of
the royal icing pale peach, place in a
piping (pastry) bag fitted with a medium
star nozzle (tube) and pipe elongated
shells, see page 38, up the sides of the
cake.

Colour 3 tablespoonsful of the remaining royal icing deep peach, fill into a bag fitted with a fine writing nozzle (tube), pipe shallow loops around the top edge of the cake. Pipe a second row under the first.

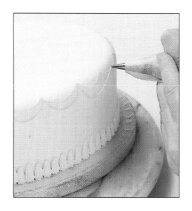

Pipe 3 small dots in between each pair of loops.

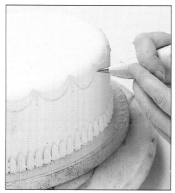

Colour small amounts of the remaining royal icing as desired and work a brush embroidery motif, see page 48.

Place the remaining pale peach royal icing in a bag fitted with a medium writing nozzle (tube) and pipe an inscription on the cake. Using the bag of deep peach icing, overpipe the inscription.

Makes one 20 cm (8 in) oval cake.

——————— CLOWN CAKE ———————

two 20 cm (8 in) round Victoria Sandwich Cakes,
    see page 12, or Whisked Sponge Cakes, see
    page 13
15 cm (6 in) square Victoria Sandwich Cake, see
    page 12, or Whisked Sponge Cake, see page 13
125 g (4 oz/ ½ cup) Buttercream, see page 14
Quick Sugarpaste, see page 20
edible green, red, yellow, brown and orange paste
    food colourings
185 g (6 oz/3/4 cup) Royal Icing, see page 22

Sandwich the two round cakes together
using 125 g (4 oz/¹/₂ cup) buttercream. Cut
a piece off one side. The flat edge should
measure approximately 13 cm (5 in.)

Spread 125 g (4 oz/½ cup) over outside of
cake. Colour 500 g (1 lb) sugarpaste pale
pink and use to cover cake, see page 20.
Mark halfway along one side of the 15 cm
(6 in) cake. Using this mark as a guide cut
cake into a triangle. Spread 85 g (3 oz/¹/₃
cup) buttercream over cake, then turn the
two side pieces to fit on top. Spread the
remaining buttercream over cake. Colour
three quarters of the sugarpaste green and
use to cover the triangle. Place the two
cake on a cakeboard, 36 cm x 31 cm (14
x 12 in).

Colour 55 g (2 oz/¹/₄ cup) sugarpaste red and use 9 walnut size pieces to form a ball for the nose.

Form the remaining red sugarpaste into two lips and attach to the cake with cooled boiled water.

Colour 30 g (1 oz) sugarpaste yellow. Roll out thinly and cut two 2.5 cm (1 in) squares.   Attach to the cake with cooled boiled water for the eyes. Colour 2 tablespoons royal icing brown, place in a piping (pastry) bag with a medium writing nozzle (tube) and pipe a cross on each eye.

Colour remaining royal icing orange, place in a piping (pastry) bag with a fine star nozzle (tube) and pipe in the hair. Form remaining sugarpaste into small balls and attach to the hat. Using food colouring paint in pink 'cheeks'.

Makes one 28 cm (11 in) high cake.

SAILING CAKE

250 g (8 oz/1 cup) Buttercream, see page 14
750 g (1 ¹/₂ lb) Quick Sugarpaste, see page 20
red, yellow, blue, green, peach and brown food
    colouring pens and edible liquid food
    colourings
185 g (6 oz/³/₄ cup) Royal Icing, see page 22

Sandwich cakes together with 125 g (4 oz/½ cup) buttercream. Spread remainder over cake and cover with sugarpaste, see page 20. Allow to dry overnight. Draw the design on the cake with food colouring pens or trace a suitable design onto greaseproof (waxed) paper and transfer to the cake surface with a craftknife.

Using a fine paintbrush and liquid food colouring, paint in the main areas of the design.

Paint in the fine details.

Colour 4 tablespoonsful royal icing blue and place in a bag fitted with a fine nozzle (tube). Pipe small loops along the side of the cake.

Pipe a second row of loops under the first row and finish with a dot above each loop.

Colour the remaining royal icing pale blue, fill a piping bag fitted with a medium star nozzle (tube) and pipe elongated shells up the side of the cake. With the bag with the fine nozzle (tube), pipe loops across the tops of alternate shells.

Makes one 20 cm (8 in) round cake.

DRUM

three 20 cm (8 in) round Victoria Sandwich
   Cakes, see page 12, or Whisked Sponge
   Cakes, see page 13
375 g (12 oz) Buttercream, see page 14
750 g (1½ lb) Quick Sugarpaste, see page 20

Decoration:
250 g (8 oz) Quick Sugarpaste, see page 20
185 g (6 oz) Royal Icing, see page 22
edible red, yellow and brown paste food
   colourings
cooled boiled water

Using half of the buttercream, sandwich
the cakes together.

Cover with remaining buttercream, see
page 15, cover with Quick Sugarpaste 20.
For the decoration, knead red colouring
into 185 g (6 oz) Quick Sugarpaste. On a
surface dusted with icing (confectioner's)
sugar, roll out to a thin rectangle 6.5 cm
(2½ in) wide and 65 cm (26 in) long.
Trim edges and cut lengthwise to make 2
strips. Place around cake, sealing ends
with cooled boiled water. Colour royal
icing yellow. Place 4 tablespoonsful in a
piping (pastry) bag fitted with a medium
writing nozzle (tube) and pipe the ropes,
see page 38, around sides of the drum.

Place the remaining yellow icing in a bag
fitted with a medium star nozzle (tube)
and pipe a large rope border, see page
38, around the top of the cake. Knead
brown food colouring into the remaining
sugarpaste and form into two drumsticks
about 10 cm (4 in) long and 8 mm (¼ in)
in diameter. Place on the cake.

Makes one 20 cm (8 in) cake.

—— MAN'S BIRTHDAY CAKE ——

20 cm (8 in) hexagonal Rich Fruit Cake, see
    page 11
750 g (1 ½ lb) Almond Paste, see page 16
4 tablespoons apricot jam, boiled, sieved and
    cooled
500 g (1 lb) Quick Sugarpaste, see page 20
icing (confectioner's) sugar for dusting
edible yellow paste food colouring

Decoration:
125 g (4 oz) Quick Sugarpaste, see page 20
edible yellow paste food colouring
icing (confectioner's) sugar for dusting
cooled boiled water
14 cm (5 in) round Cocoa Painted Plaque, see
    page 46

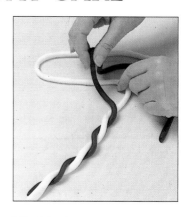

Cover cake with almond paste, see page 17. Knead yellow food colouring into Quick Sugarpaste to colour it cream, use to cover the cake, see page 20. For the decoration, knead a little yellow colouring into the Quick Sugarpaste to colour it cream. Divide in half and colour one portion dark brown. On a surface lightly dusted with icing (confectioner's) sugar, using your hands, roll each half to a thin sausage 67.5 cm (27 in) long, twist together to form a rope; if the 'sausages' break, do not worry as they can be butted together when placed around cake.

Using a little cooled boiled water, attach the rope to the base of cake. Using a little royal icing, attach the plaque to the cake. Colour half the royal icing cream, place in a piping (pastry) bag fitted with a medium writing nozzle (tube) and pipe the inscription on the cake. Colour the remaining icing dark brown, transfer to a bag fitted with a fine writing nozzle (tube) and over-pipe the inscription.

Makes one 20 cm (8 in) cake.

——— NEW YEAR CAKE ———

two 20 cm (8 in) shallow square Victoria
    Sandwich Cakes, see page 12, or Whisked
    Sponge Cakes, see page 13
250 g (8 oz) Buttercream, see page 14
500 g (1 lb) Quick Sugarpaste, see page 20
icing (confectioner's) sugar for dusting
250 g (8 oz) Royal Icing without glycerine, see
    Note
edible blue and yellow paste food colourings
375 g (12 oz) Royal Icing, see page 22

Using half of the buttercream, sandwich
the cakes together, then cover using the
remaining buttercream. Cover with the
Quick Sugarpaste, see page 20.

For the run-outs see page 54, making the
templates by drawing the outlines of 2
bells approximately 7.5 cm (3 in) high.
Colour 2 tablespoonsful of the royal icing
without glycerine blue, place in a bag
fitted with a fine writing nozzle (tube)
and pipe the outline for run-outs. Thin-
down the remaining royal icing without
glycerine and fill in the outlines, see page
54. Leave to dry for 24 hours.

Place 4 tablespoonsful royal icing in a bag fitted with a small star nozzle (tube) and pipe a small C-scroll border around the top of the cake, see page 39. Place 4 tablespoonsful of white icing in a bag fitted with medium writing nozzle (tube) and piped dropped lines along the sides of the cake, approximately half-way up.

Colour 115 g (4 oz) royal icing blue and place half in a bag fitted with a fine writing nozzle (tube) and overpipe the C-scroll, see page 39. Colour 115 g (4 oz) royal icing yellow and place half in a bag fitted with a fine writing nozzle (tube) and pipe a row of yellow dots above the side lines, and 3 graduated dots down the side of the cake between the scallops.

Carefully remove the run-outs from the paper and attach to the cake using a little royal icing. Place the remaining blue icing in a bag fitted with a small petal tube. Tilting the nozzle (tube), pipe a bow at the top of the bells so that it stands out. Place the remaining yellow icing in a bag fitted with a small petal nozzle (tube), pipe a smaller bow inside the first. Using the bag of white icing fitted with a fine star nozzle (tube), pipe shells around the bottom of the cake.

Using the bag of white icing fitted with a fine star nozzle (tube), pipe a row of shells around the base of the cake. Using the bag of blue icing fitted with a fine writing nozzle (tube), pipe dots between each shell.

Makes one 20 cm (8 in) square cake.

Note: This is made in the same way as royal icing, see page 22, except that glycerine is omitted from the ingredients.

CHRISTMAS CAKE

20 cm (8 in) hexagonal Rich Fruit Cake, see
    page 11
875 g (1³/₄ lb) Almond Paste, see page 16
4 tablespoons apricot jam, boiled, sieved and
    cooled
icing (confectioner's) sugar for dusting
875 g (1³/₄ lb) Quick Sugarpaste, see page 20

Decoration:
375 g (12 oz) Quick Sugarpaste, see page 20
edible red, brown and yellow paste food
    colourings
icing (confectioner's) sugar for dusting
cooled boiled water

Cover the cake with almond paste, see
page 17, and Quick Sugarpaste, see page
20. For the decoration, to make choirboys, knead red food colouring into 250
g (8 oz) of the Quick Sugarpaste. Divide into four pieces of slightly differing
sizes. Mould into cone shapes. From
the remaining red sugarpaste, mould 8
small tapered pieces for the 'arms'. Using
cooled boiled water, attach to the 'bodies'.

On a surface lightly dusted with icing (confectioner's) sugar, roll out half of the remaining Quick Sugarpaste to a very thin circle. Using a 4 cm (1½ in) fluted biscuit (cookie) cutter, cut out four circles. Using a cocktail stick, frill around the edges, see page 50. Using cooled boiled water, attach to the 'bodies'.

Using a little red food colouring, colour the remaining sugarpaste pink. Break off 4 pieces and roll into small balls for the 'heads' and attach to the bodies using cooled boiled water. Make 8 very small balls for the 'hands'. Attach to the bodies using cooled boiled water. Leave to dry overnight.

Colour 2 tablespoons royal icing dark brown, and 2 tablespoons yellow. Using separate piping (pastry) bags fitted with fine writing nozzles (tubes), pipe in 'hair' on each 'head'. Using food colouring pens or a fine paintbrush, paint in faces with different expressions.

Colour half the royal icing green and place in a bag fitted with a fine writing nozzle. Pipe a spray of holly leaves. Colour the remaining royal icing red and place in a bag fitted with a fine writing nozzle, pipe in the holly berries. Place the choirboys in position and attach ribbon round the sides of the cake with a little royal icing.

Makes one 20 cm (8 in) hexagonal cake.

CHRISTMAS CAKE

250 g (8 oz) Buttercream, see page 14
two 20 cm (8 in) round Victoria Sandwich
    Cakes, see page 12, or Whisked Sponge
    Cakes, see page 13
500 g (1 lb) Quick Sugarpaste, see page 20
310 g (10 oz) Royal Icing, see page 22
edible red and green paste food colourings

Using half of the buttercream, sandwich
the cakes then cover with the remainder.
Cover with the Quick Sugarpaste, see
page 20.

Make a greaseproof (waxed) paper
template of a star, see page 52, place on
the cake and mark the outline on the cake
by cutting through with a craft knife or
fine, sharp knife. Place 4 tablespoonsful
of the royal icing in a piping (pastry) bag
fitted with a medium writing nozzle (tube),
pipe the star outline. Colour 4
tablespoonsful of the royal icing red, place
in a bag fitted with a fine writing nozzle
(tube) and pipe dots inside the star.

Colour 4 tablespoonsful of the icing green, place in a bag fitted with a fine writing nozzle (tube) and pipe holly leaves inside each star point. Using the bag of red icing, pipe in holly berries.

Place the remaining icing in a bag fitted with a medium star nozzle (tube) and pipe scrolls, see page 39, around the top edge of the cake.

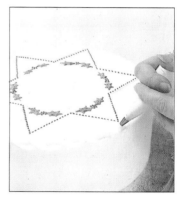

Using the bag of red icing, overpipe the scrolls. Then pipe a scalloped rope, see page 38, over the shells.

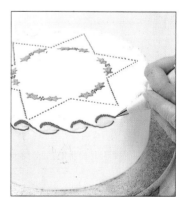

Using the bag filled with white royal icing and the medium star tube, pipe shells round the base of the cake. Pipe a scalloped rope over the shells using the red royal icing. Attach a 0.75 metre (30 in) length of yellow ribbon using a little royal icing.

Makes one 20 cm (8 in) round cake.

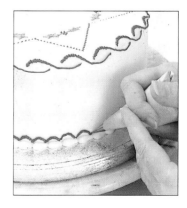

— CHRISTMAS CANDLE CAKE —

two 20 cm (8 in) Victoria Sandwich Cakes, see
   page 12, or Whisked Sponge Cakes, see
   page 13
250 g (8 oz) Buttercream, see page 14
750 g (1 ½ lb) Quick Sugarpaste, see page 20
edible green, red and yellow paste food colourings
2 tablespoons Royal Icing, see page 22

Sandwich cakes together using half the
buttercream. Spread remainder over outside of cake. Colour 500 g (1 lb) Quick
Sugarpaste pale green and cover cake.
Colour 185 g (6 oz/³/₄ cup) sugarpaste red.
Reserve 2 tablespoonsful; mould 3 different
size candles. Leave to dry completely.

Break off a walnut size piece of the
remaining sugarpaste and colour yellow.
Mould 3 small flames.

Stick the candles to the cake using a little
royal icing.

Colour the remaining sugarpaste green.
Roll out very thinly and cut out holly
leaves.

Using a little royal icing, attach leaves
around the base of the candles.

Cut out more holly leaves as required and
attach around the base of the cake.
Mould the reserved red sugarpaste into
small berries and attach amongst the
leaves. Attach the flames to the tops of
the candles.

Makes one 20 cm (8 in) round cake.

RETIREMENT CAKE

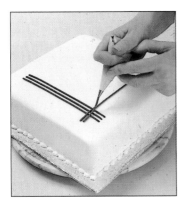

250 g (8 oz) Buttercream, see page 14
two 20 cm (8 in) square Victoria Sandwich Cakes,
    see page 12, or Whisked Sponge Cakes, see
    page 13
500 g (1 lb) Quick Sugarpaste, see page 20
icing (confectioner's) sugar for dusting
345 g (11 oz) Royal Icing, see page 22
edible brown, green, red, orange, yellow and blue
    paste food colourings

Using half of the buttercream, sandwich
the cakes together, then cover with the
remaining buttercream. Cover with the
Quick Sugarpaste, see page 20.

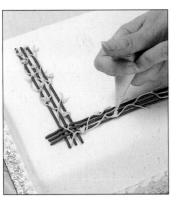

Colour 2 tablespoonsful of the royal icing
dark brown. Place in a piping (pastry) bag
fitted with a thick writing nozzle (tube),
pipe 3 straight lines along one side of the
top of the cake. Turn the cake and pipe
another 3 lines. Place 4 tablespoons royal
icing in a bag fitted with a medium star
nozzle (tube) and pipe shells round the
base of the cake.

Colour 4 tablespoonsful of the royal icing green; place half in a bag fitted with a medium writing nozzle (tube). Pipe in the vines. Put the remaining green icing in a greaseproof (waxed) paper piping (pastry) bag without either the point cut off or a nozzle (tube). Cut the end of the bag in a 'V' shape and pipe leaves along the vines, see page 42.

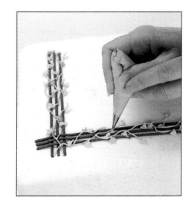

Colour 2 tablespoonsful royal icing pink, 2 tablespoonsful orange and 2 tablespoonsful yellow. Each time using a bag fitted with a fine writing nozzle (tube), pipe pink, orange and yellow flowers at random along the vines.

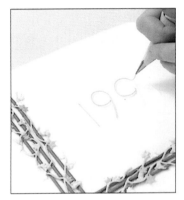

Colour the remaining icing blue, place in a bag fitted with a fine writing nozzle (tube), pipe a double loop border around the top edge of the cake.   Place 2 tablespoonsful of white royal icing in a bag fitted with a medium writing nozzle (tube), and pipe an inscription.   Overpipe, using the bag of blue icing fitted with a fine writing nozzle (tube).

With the bag of green icing and the medium writing nozzle (tube) pipe grass up the sides of the cake. Pipe flowers in the grass with the bags of pink, orange and yellow icing.

Makes one 20 cm (8 in) round cake.

—— ENGAGEMENT CAKE ——

20 cm (8 in) heart-shaped Rich Fruit Cake, see
    page 11
1 kg (2 lb) Almond Paste, see page 16
4 tablespoons apricot jam, boiled, sieved and
    cooled
750 g (1½ lb) Royal Icing, see page 22
edible pink paste food colouring
icing (confectioner's) sugar for dusting

Decoration:
250 g (8 oz) Royal Icing, see page 22
Moulded Carnations, see page 32

Cover the Cake with Almond Paste, see
page 17.

Using a little red colouring, colour the
royal icing pale pink then cover the cake,
see page 22. For the decoration, make a
greaseproof (waxed) paper template for
the sides of the cake, see page 52. Place
on the cake. Using a craft knife, mark the
pattern. Remove the template. Tilt the
cake by placing it on an upturned
basin covered with a cloth. Colour 4
tablespoons of the royal icing deep pink.
Place in a piping (pastry) bag fitted with a
fine writing nozzle (tube) and pipe a tiny
scallop pattern along the marked line.

Using the same bag, pipe a bow in each
large scallop. Colour the remaining royal
icing pale pink. Place in a bag fitted with
a medium star nozzle (tube) and pipe a
fancy shell border in a herringbone pattern along the top edge of the cake. Pipe
shells down the front and around the base
of the cake. Using a little royal icing, attach the moulded carnations.

Makes one 20 cm (8 in) heart-shaped cake.

STAR CAKE

two 20 cm (8 in) round Victoria Sandwich Cakes,
  see page 12, or Whisked Sponge Cakes, see
  page 13
750 g (1 ½ lb) Buttercream, see page 14
icing (confectioner's) sugar for dusting
55 g (2 oz) Quick Sugarpaste, see page 20
blue and yellow edible paste food colourings
55 g (2 oz) Royal Icing, see page 22

Using 85 g (3 oz) buttercream, sandwich
cakes together, spread 85 g (3 oz) over the
cake. With the aid of a template, mark
top edge of cake into 6 sections.

Colour ¹/₆ remaining buttercream blue,
transfer to a piping (pastry) bag fitted with
a medium star nozzle (tube) and pipe stars
along the marked lines and around the
base of the cake. Colour ¹/₃ of the remaining buttercream yellow, place in a bag
fitted with a small star nozzle (tube) and
pipe star to fill the star pattern. Fill the
remaining buttercream into a bag fitted
with a medium star nozzle (tube) and
cover the remainder of the cake with
stars.

On a surface lightly dusted with icing
(confectioner's) sugar, roll out the sugarpaste to 3mm (¹/₈ in) thick. Using a 10 cm
(4 in) fluted cutter, cut out a circle. Leave
to dry. Colour the royal icing blue and
place in a piping (pastry) bag fitted with a
fine writing nozzle (tube). Pipe the inscription of your choice. Place on the cake.

Makes one 20 cm (8 in) cake.

—— WEDDING CAKE ——

20 cm (8 in) and 25 cm (10 in) heart-shaped
    Victoria Sandwich Cakes, see page 12, or
    Whisked Sponge Cakes, see page 13
2.4 kg (4 lb) Almond Paste, see page 16
icing (confectioner's) sugar for dusting
10 tablespoons apricot jam, boiled, sieved and
    cooled
edible yellow paste food colouring
1.75 kg (3 ½ lb) Royal Icing, see page 22

Decoration:
440 g (14 oz) Royal Icing, see page 22
edible yellow paste food colouring
deep pink Moulded Roses, see page 34

Cover the cakes with almond paste, see
page 16, using 875 g (1 lb) for the smaller
one and the rest for the other. Add a little
yellow food colouring into the royal icing
to colour it cream, then use to cover the
cakes, using 500 g (1 lb) for the smaller
one and the rest for the other. For
the decoration, add a little yellow food
colouring to the royal icing to colour it
cream. Divide each side of the cakes into
6 and mark a scallop on the side of each
cake. Mark a corresponding scallop on
the top of the smaller cake.

Place the small cake on a 20 cm (8 in) heart-shaped thin cake card and position it towards the back of the large cake. Place 4 tablespoonsful of the royal icing in a piping (pastry) bag fitted with a medium star nozzle (tube), and pipe a row of shells around the bottom of both tiers.

Using the rope technique, see page 38, pipe along the curved lines, graduating the size of the rope so that it is larger in the centre and tapering at the ends.

Pipe a large star where the scallops join. Add more icing to the bag as necessary. Place 4 tablespoonsful of the icing in a bag fitted with a medium writing nozzle (tube) and pipe double rows of dropped loops under the ropes on the cake sides and pipe similar loops on the cake top. Using a little royal icing, attach the moulded roses.

Place an ornament on top of the cake and surround with moulded roses.

Makes one 2-tier heart-shaped cake.

WEDDING CAKE

15 cm (6 in), 20 cm (8 in) and 25 cm (10 in)
  round Rich Fruit Cakes, see page 11
2.5 kg (5 lb) Almond Paste, see page 16
approximately 250 g (8 oz) apricot jam, boiled,
  sieved and cooled
2.65 kg (5 lb) Quick Sugarpaste, see page 20

Decoration:
250 g (8 oz) Royal Icing, see page 22
edible coral paste food colourings
cooled boiled water
750 g (1 ½ lb) Quick Sugarpaste, see page 20

Cover cakes with almond paste and sugarpaste, see pages 17/20, using 375 g (12 oz)
almond paste and 500 g (1 lb) sugarpaste for the smallest cake, 875 g (1³/₄ lb)
each almond paste and sugarpaste for the
medium and 1.25 kg (2½ lb) each almond
paste and sugarpaste for the largest. For
the decoration, place 125 g (4 oz) royal
icing in a piping (pastry) bag fitted with a
star nozzle (tube) and pipe shells around
base of each cake.

Mix coral colouring into 85 g (3 oz) of remaining royal icing, place in a bag fitted with a fine writing nozzle (tube) and pipe small dots on sides of cakes. In a surface lightly dusted with icing (confectioner's) sugar, roll out half of the Quick Sugarpaste to a circle about 7.5 cm (3 in) larger than the largest cake. Trim the edges and add the trimmings to the remaining sugarpaste.

Lightly brush the top of the cake with cooled boiled water to moisten, and place the sugarpaste circle on top and arrange the sides in folds to resemble a tablecloth. Use ²/₃ of the remaining sugarpaste to cover the middle-sized cake, and the remainder to cover the small cake. Reserve the trimmings.

Using the bag of coral icing, pipe a small scallop pattern around the edge of the sugarpaste overlay, see page 38. Colour the reserved sugarpaste to match the coral royal icing and roll out very thinly. Using either a tiny biscuit, or aspic cutter, cut out about 50 small flower shapes. Roll the edges to frill them, see page 50. Place on a piece of foam and carefully press down on the centres so they cup slightly. Allow to dry.

Using a little royal icing, attach the flowers at random; leave to dry. Colour the remaining royal icing yellow, transfer to a piping (pastry) bag fitted with a fine writing nozzle (tube), pipe tiny dots in the centre of each flower. At the reception, place flowers or an ornament on the cake as desired.

Makes one 3-tier wedding cake.

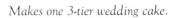

——— CHRISTENING CAKE ———

20 cm (8 in) oval Rich Fruit Cake, see page 11
750 g (1 ½ lb) Almond Paste, see page 16
4 tablespoons apricot jam, boiled, sieved and
    cooled
icing (confectioner's) sugar for dusting
500 g (1 lb) Quick Sugarpaste, see page 20

Decoration:
icing (confectioner's) sugar for dusting
125 g (4 oz) Quick Sugarpaste, see page 20
185 g (6 oz) royal icing, see page 22
cooled boiled water
edible red paste food colouring

Cover the cake with almond paste, see page 17, and Quick Sugarpaste, see page 20. For the decoration, mark a line 4 cm (1 in) from the base of the cake and attach a 0.75 metre (30 in) length of 3 mm (¹/₈ in) wide pink ribbon around the cake, using fine dots of royal icing. Fill a piping (pastry) bag fitted with a small star nozzle (tube) with half the royal icing and pipe shells around the base.

On a surface lightly dusted with icing (confectioner's) sugar, very thinly roll out half of the Quick Sugarpaste and cut out about 14 circles using a 5 cm (2 in) fluted biscuit cutter. Frill each circle with a cocktail stick, see page 50, and cut in half.

Using a special cutter, or small flower cutter, cut eyelet holes in each semi-circle. Using a little cooled boiled water, attach frills to the side of the cake. Place 4 tablespoons of the royal icing into a piping (pastry) bag fitted with a medium writing nozzle (tube) and pipe shells along the top of the frills.

Colour half the remaining royal icing pink, fill a piping (pastry) bag fitted with a fine writing nozzle (tube), and pipe around the eyelet holes. Pipe an embroidery pattern, see page 47, above the ribbon.

Make a greaseproof (waxed) pattern to resemble a baby's bib. Roll out the remaining sugarpaste and cut around the pattern. Frill around the edge with a cocktail stick, see page 50; leave to dry completely. Fill a piping (pastry) bag fitted with a medium writing nozzle (tube), pipe an inscription on the bib, if desired, and attach to cake top with a little royal icing.

Makes one 20 cm (8 in) round cake.

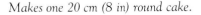

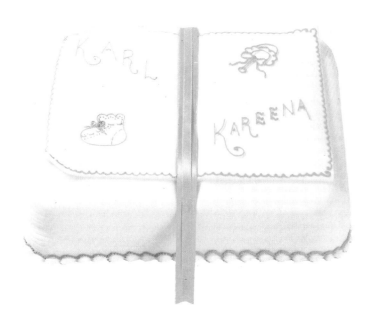

— TWINS CHRISTENING CAKE —

two 25 x 20 cm (10 x 8 in) Victoria Sandwich
   see page 12, or Whisked Sponge Cakes, see
   page 13
375 g (12 oz) Buttercream, see page 14
750 g (1 ½ lb) Quick Sugarpaste, see page 20
icing (confectioner's) sugar for dusting
cooled boiled water
155 g (5 oz) royal icing, see page 22

Using half of the buttercream, sandwich
the two cakes together; trim to a book
shape curving the corners and cutting a
'V' down the centre. Spread the remaining buttercream over the outside of the
cake.

Cover the cake with 750 g (1¹/₂ lb) of the
sugarpaste, see page 20. Using a cocktail
stick, score the sides of the cake to represent the pages of a book.

On a surface lightly dusted with icing (confectioner's) sugar, thinly roll the remaining sugarpaste to a rectangle to fit the top of the cake; trim the edges. Fix to top with a little cooled boiled water and and prop up the corners with small pieces of absorbent kitchen paper.

Place 4 tablespoonsful of the royal icing in a piping (pastry) bag fitted with a small star nozzle (tube) and pipe shells around the base. Place 2 tablespoonsful of the royal icing in a bag fitted with medium writing nozzle (tube), and pipe the babies' names on the cake, then pipe motifs on each page.

Colour half of the remaining royal icing blue and half pink, or according to the sex of the children. Place separately in bags fitted with a fine writing nozzle (tube) and overpipe the names and motifs.

Pipe a small rope design round the edges of the pages and above the base shells. Using small dots of royal icing, attach ribbons to resemble book marks.

Makes one 20 cm (8 in) oblong cake.

—— SILVER WEDDING CAKE ——

20 cm (8 in) petal-shaped Rich Fruit Cake, see
    page 11
750 g (1 ½ lb) Almond Paste, see page 16
4 tablespons apricot jam, boiled sieved and
    cooled
500 g (1 lb) Quick Sugarpaste, see page 20

Decoration:
250 g (8 oz) Quick Sugarpaste, see page 20
125 g (4 oz) Royal Icing, see page 22
edible silver paste food colouring

Cover the cake with the almond paste, see
page 17, then with sugarpaste, see page
20. Using a paper template, see page 52,
mark curved lines on each of the cake
curves. Place half the royal icing in a
piping (pastry) bag fitted with a small star
nozzle (tube) and pipe small shells around
the base of the cake.

Using half of the Quick Sugarpaste, make 12 Garrett Frills, see page 50. Attach in 2 rows   along the marked lines, positioning the second frill about 5 mm (¼ in) above the first.

Place the remaining royal icing in a bag fitted with a fine writing nozzle (tube), pipe tiny shells along the joins. Then pipe an embroidery motif.

Using edible silver food colouring and a fine paintbrush, paint the edges of the frills.

Using a little royal icing, attach silver banding to the edge of the cake board and position an ornament or flowers as desired.

Makes one 20 cm (8 in) petal-shaped cake.

— GOLDEN WEDDING CAKE —

20 cm (8 in) square Rich Fruit Cake, see page 11
1 kg (2 lb) Almond Paste, see page 16
4 tablespoons apricot jam, boiled, sieved and
    cooled
1.25 kg (2½ lb) Royal Icing, see page 22
edible yellow paste food colouring

Decoration
440 g (14 oz) Royal Icing, see page 22
edible yellow paste food colouring
2 Sugar Bells, see page 26

Cover the cake with almond paste, see
page 17. Colour the royal icing pale yellow, then cover the cake, see page 22.
For the decoration, make a greaseproof
(waxed) paper template for the top of the
cake, see page 52.

Place on the cake and mark around the outline with a craft knife or fine-bladed, sharp knife. Colour 375 g (12 oz) royal icing pale yellow to match the icing on the cake. Place 4 tablespoonsful into a piping (pastry) bag fitted with a medium writing nozzle (tube) and pipe over the marked line.

Place a further 2 tablespoons pale yellow royal icing into a bag fitted with a fine writing nozzle (tube) and pipe a continuous squiggly line between the piped outline and the edge of the cake.

Place another 4 tablespoonsful of the icing into a bag fitted with a medium star nozzle (tube) and pipe scrolls, see page 39, along the top edges of the cake. Using a little royal icing, attach two 0.9 metre (36 in) lengths of gold ribbon around the sides of the cake.

Using the bag with the medium star nozzle (tube), pipe shells down the corners and around the base. Colour the remaining royal icing deep yellow. Place half into a bag fitted with a fine writing nozzle (tube) and overpipe the pattern outline and the scrolls. Using a little royal icing, attach the sugar bells and finish with a bow of gold ribbon.

Makes one 20 cm (8 in) square cake.

RICH FRUIT CAKE

Ingredients	Cake size	Cake Size
	15 cm (6 in) round 13 cm (5 in) square	25 cm (10 cm) 23 cm (9 in)
currants	250 g (8 oz/1⅔ cups)	625 g (1¼ lb/4 cups)
sultanas	125 g (4 oz/¾ cup)	315 g (10 oz/2 cups)
raisins	125 g (4 oz/¾ cup)	315 g (10 oz/2 cups)
flaked almonds	30 g (1 oz/2 tbs)	85 g (3 oz/½ cup)
candied mixed peel	30 g (1 oz/⅓ cup)	85 g (3 oz/¾ cup)
glacé cherries, chopped	55 g (2 oz/⅓ cup)	125 g (4 oz/¾ cup)
lemons, grated rind and juice	½	1½
sherry	1 tablespoon	3 tablespoons
butter	125 g (4 oz/½ cup)	345 g (11 oz/2⅔ cups)
soft brown sugar	125 g (4 oz/1 cup)	345 g (11 oz/2⅔ cups)
plain (all-purpose) flour	125 g (4 oz/1 cup)	325 g (11 oz/2⅔ cups)
mixed spice	½ teaspoon	1½ teaspoons
eggs, beaten	2	6
baking temperature	135C (275F/Gas 1)	135C (275F/Gas 1)
time	2¼-3 hours	6 hours

VICTORIA SANDWICH CAKE

Ingredients	Cake size	Cake Size
	15 cm (6 in) round 13 cm (5 in) square	25 cm (10 cm) 23 cm (9 in)
butter	125 g (4 oz/½ cup)	250 g (8 oz/1 cup)
caster (superfine) sugar	125 g (4 oz/½ cup)	250 g (8 oz/1 cup)
eggs	2	4
plain (all-purpose) flour	125 g (4 oz/1 cup)	250 g (8 oz/2 cups)
baking temperature	180C (350F/Gas 4)	180C (350F/Gas 4)
time	50-60 minutes	1 hour

WHISKED SPONGE CAKE

Ingredients	Cake size	Cake Size
	15 cm (6 in) round 13 cm (5 in) square	25 cm (10 cm) 23 cm (9 in)
eggs	2	4
caster (superfine) sugar	55 g (2 oz/¼ cup)	125 g (4 oz/½ cup)
plain (all-purpose) flour	55 g (2 oz/½ cup)	125 g (4 oz/1 cup)
baking temperature	180C (350F/Gas 4)	180C (350F/Gas 4)
time	20 minutes	35 minutes

ALMOND PASTE

Ingredients	Yield		
	250 g (8 oz)	500 g (1 lb)	825 g (1½ lb)
ground almonds	125 g (4 oz/1¼ cups)	250 g (8 oz/2¼ cups)	375 g (12 oz/3¾ cups)
caster (superfine) sugar	55 g (2 oz/¼ cup)	125 g (4 oz/½ cup)	185 g (6 oz/¾ cup)
icing (confectioner's) sugar	55 g (2 oz/⅓ cup)	125 g (4 oz/¾ cup)	185 g (6 oz/1 cup)
egg yolks	1	2	3
lemon juice	½ teaspoon	½ teaspoon	1 teaspoon

QUICK SUGARPASTE

Ingredients	Yield		
	250 g (8 oz)	500 g (1 lb)	750 g (1½ lb)
icing (confectioner's) sugar, sifted	250 g (8 oz/½ cup)	500 g (1 lb/3 cups)	750 g (1½ lb/4½ cups)
egg white	½	1	1½

ROYAL ICING

Ingredients	Yield		
	250 g (8 oz)	500 g (1 lb)	750 g (1½ lb)
icing (confectioner's) sugar, sifted	210 g (7 oz/1½ cups)	420 g (14 oz/3 cups)	630 g (21 oz/4½ cups)
egg white	1	2	3

ABCDE
FGHIJ
KLMNO
PQRST
UVWXY
Z

Lettering stencil

Border and Edge templates

INDEX